CASE STUDIES IN
EDUCATION AND CULTURE

———

General Editors
GEORGE *and* LOUISE SPINDLER
Stanford University

———

ALASKAN ESKIMO EDUCATION
A Film Analysis of Cultural Confrontation in the Schools

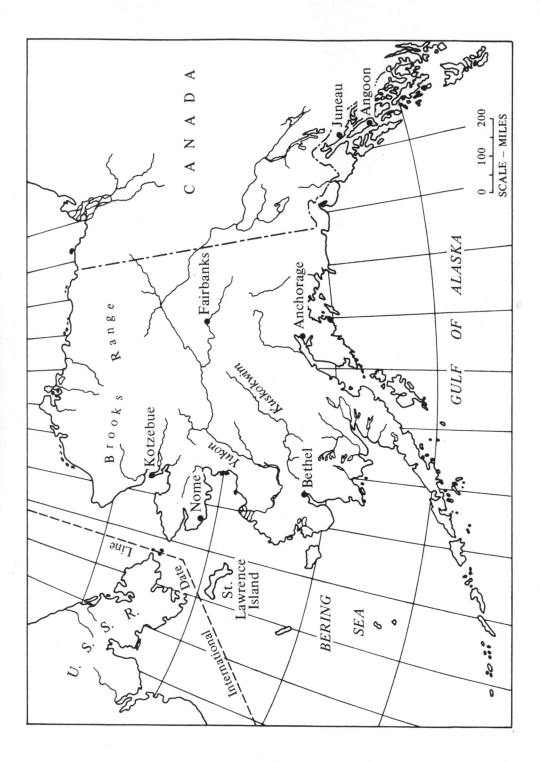

ALASKAN ESKIMO EDUCATION

EDUCATION

A Film Analysis of Cultural Confrontation in the Schools

JOHN COLLIER, JR.
California State University

HOLT, RINEHART AND WINSTON, INC.

New York • Chicago • San Francisco • Atlanta
Dallas • Montreal • Toronto • London • Sydney

*To John Connelly
for His Enthusiasm and
Faith in Education*

Copyright © 1973 by Holt, Rinehart and Winston, Inc.
All rights reserved
Library of Congress Catalog Card Number: 72–90649
ISBN: 0–03–088021–1
Printed in the United States of America
3 4 5 6   059   9 8 7 6 5 4 3 2 1

Foreword

ABOUT THE SERIES

This series brings to students the results of direct observation and participation in educational process, by anthropologists, in a variety of cultural settings, including some within the contemporary United States. Each of the books in this series is selected as an enduring example of educational anthropology. Classrooms, schools, communities and their schools, cultural transmission in societies where there are no schools in the Western sense, all are represented in the series. The authors of these studies move beyond formalistic treatments of institutions to the interaction among the people engaged in educative events, their thinking and feeling, and to the educative transactions themselves.

Education is a cultural process. Every act of teaching and learning is a cultural event. Education recruits new members into society and maintains the culture. Education may also be an instrument for change as new adaptations are disseminated.

Generalizations about relationships between schools and communities, education and society, and education and culture become meaningful when education is studied as a cultural process. This series is intended for use in courses in education, and in anthropology and the other social sciences, where these relationships are particularly relevant. They will stimulate thinking and discussion about education that is not confined by one's own cultural experience. The cross-cultural emphasis of the series is particularly significant. Without this perspective, our view will be obscured by ethnocentric bias.

ABOUT THE AUTHOR

John Collier's qualifications are those of a fieldworker and an observer of culture. In his role as photographer he has brought special sensitivity to recognition and recording of the field circumstance.

Collier's first fieldwork was in the early forties with the Farm Security Administration photographic team led by Roy E. Stryker. Here, working with Edwin Rosskam, Arthur Rothstein, John Vachon, Jack Delano, and Russell Lee, Collier was educated in the social and economic content of the documentary visual record. When Stryker moved from government to industry, much of his staff moved with him, and Collier spent four roving years recording the role of petroleum as an agent of change, from the arctic to the tropics. This experience brought him to the challenge of cultural significance in photographic imagery.

In 1946 Collier collaborated with Anibal Buitron, Ecuadorean anthropologist, in an experimental study to record with the camera the complexity of culture and processes of change. *The Awakening Valley*, by Collier and Buitron, reported on this effort of combining photography and ethnography.

From this point Collier moved directly into anthropology. For three years he worked as a research assistant with Dr. Alexander H. Leighton, of Cornell University, exploring and testing out various photographic methodologies that could open the door to the nonverbal content of culture. These studies included cross-cultural fieldwork in the Maritimes of Canada and the Navajo Reservation. Next Collier worked for a year assembling for Dr. Allan R. Holmberg a photographic baseline of the culture of Vicos against which to evaluate change in the Peru-Cornell Project. A comprehensive photographic ethnography was prepared, which awaits publication.

For the past ten years Collier has devoted his time to teaching and research in visual anthropology. He has worked consistently in the area of acculturation and the welfare of American Indians and more recently in problems of Indian education. After his film study of Alaskan Eskimos, Collier continued this educational research in the Rough Rock Demonstration School in Arizona.

Collier has lectured at Stanford University, the University of California at Berkeley and Davis, the University of Oregon, and the University of Washington. He is now an associate professor in Education and Anthropology at California State University at San Francisco and also teaches creative photography at the San Francisco Art Institute.

About the Book

This is a study of the educational process where the teacher and the student represent different communities. The settings for the study range from schools in isolated Alaskan villages attended only by Eskimos to schools in Anchorage where only 7 percent of the student body are Eskimo, Indian, and Aleutian. The research is unique not only because it was done on a wide range of communities but because it was carried out by an anthropologist using film and tape as his major data collecting devices. The procedures used and explained by John Collier in this case study enabled him in a comparatively short period of time and with twenty hours of film as data to produce a substantial and very insightful analysis of education.

Perhaps because of his use of motion picture photography as a research technique, his analysis calls attention to the elemental rhythms of interaction and movement within the classroom. The teacher who moves into and becomes a part of the circle of children, the teacher who talks to the empty seats in the classroom at a great distance, the teacher who is oriented to the individual tasks of individual children, and the children themselves, involved and spontaneous or bored and sleepy, come through in a way that is rare in the literature of schooling and education.

The insights into educational process to be gained from this case study are not limited in their application to Eskimo or Indian education alone. The teacher in every school in every classroom is in some measure separated culturally from his or her students. The separation and insulation of the teacher is more severe in the cases described by John Collier than in many schools in the United States, but the elements of interaction and communication are perceivable and held in common in all schools. Conversely, the elements of effective teaching and productive learning are identifiable and applicable to all schools. In this case study it is clear that education is a transaction dependent upon interaction and empathy.

The case study also raises questions about the relevance of what is taught. It is not merely a question of whether Eskimo children should be taught about the culture and technology of the Whiteman in, say, Seattle, Washington, but rather one of how the knowledge about Seattle shall be joined with an understanding of the environment in which the Eskimo child is living. If the teacher is sealed off from this environment both physically and psychologically, the probability that a viable joining will occur is remote. This generalization applies to any school any place.

George and Louise Spindler
General Editors
STANFORD, CALIFORNIA

Preface

Alaskan Eskimo Education: A Film Analysis of Cultural Confrontation in the Schools is an account of the drama and challenge of an ecologically bound people attempting to find a place in the modern development, or disruption, that is sweeping the Alaskan Arctic.

Briefly, it is an account of *White* education for *Brown* people as taught by White teachers imported into the Arctic. What do the White teachers have to give the Eskimos? White ways and White values? Can they also offer Native students the opportunity to embrace themselves first as Eskimos, so that later they can be effective men and women whether in their own villages or in the White-dominated world? If White teachers cannot do this, if White programming cannot teach the whole Eskimo child, *why not?* If some teachers can, *how* do they do it?

This book is not an evaluation of teachers and schools as "superior" or "inferior"; rather it is an observation of educational communication between cultures. A central element in the challenge is the environment itself. For the Eskimos the Arctic tundra world is home—difficult, but understood and accepted. For the White teachers it is alien—not only difficult, but hostile and drastically isolated from their own cultural roots. How do White teachers carry on in such isolation? And what is the impact of their presence on the Eskimo community? The White teachers' living style is seen to be as significant a part of White education as is the school curriculum.

This book is about both students and teachers attempting to work together. In the Arctic, as on the Navajo Reservation and elsewhere, we see students needing and wanting education, and teachers urgently attempting to bring it to them. We see dedicated, often very well-trained teachers putting great effort into their task of promoting the welfare of their Native students. Yet despite felt needs and great urgency, too often this schooling fails. Sometimes it may reach halfway to practical achievement. But only rarely do we find Native students, Eskimo or Indian, acquiring from their schools either the experience or the sophistication needed to survive *either* in their indigenous world or in the modern White world. Most of the students appear trapped in apprehensive suspension between cultures. Why does this happen so often, even with eager teachers? What is the nature of this failure? How does it take place? And what can be done about the human default that only an occasional teacher can remedy?

These problems are the challenge, the focus for our camera. Surely there will be clues in the film record of the school process that might describe failure when it happens and define success wherever it can be observed.

This book then does not discuss circumstances theoretically, but rather describes them concretely as recorded on film. Education, as it takes place in the classroom, is presented directly to the reader for his evaluation. The film-text attempts to focus realistically on Eskimo children as they work—or withdraw or simply pass the time—and also on their teachers. The survey attempts to cover the full range of learning environments in West Central Alaska, in two isolated tundra villages, in the trading center of Bethel, and finally in Alaska's largest city, Anchorage. Where do Eskimos learn best? And *how* do Eskimos learn best? This is our search in *Alaskan Eskimo Education*.

John Collier, Jr.

Acknowledgments

This is a study of students and teachers and administrators in Alaska, and it was made possible only because of their gracious cooperation. I wish to thank and acknowledge the generosity of all these collaborators, with particular appreciation to William Benton, director of Bureau of Indian Affairs (BIA) Education on the Bethel Area, to Roman and Litha Kinney, Henry B. Bowen, William and Judy Morgenstein, and Donald MacLowry, teachers in BIA schools; to Ida Nicori, who opened the door to the Head Start Program for me and to her father, Alexi Nicori, my host at Kwethluk; to Maxwell Fancher, superintendent of the Bethel Consolidated Schools; to James Conaway, director of elementary education in Anchorage; and special thanks to Boyd Fonnesbeck, principal in Anchorage, who offered rich insights into Native education, as well as hospitality.

The study was also made with the direct cooperation and support of the National Study of American Indian Education. I especially wish to thank its director, Robert J. Havighurst, for his imagination to see the potentialities of the film's part in the study and his generous help throughout, and its associate director, Estelle Fuchs, for her guidance in the research writing of the initial report. I am particularly indebted to my colleagues, John Connelly, regional director for the Northwest Coast and Alaska Area of the National Study, and Ray and Carol Barnhardt, who were fellow researchers with me in Bethel and who have continued to give advice and counsel on the writing.

Alyce Cathey, Paul Michaels, Mack E. Ford, and my son, Malcolm Collier, were the hardworking researchers who carried out the detailed work of viewing and analyzing the content of the films—*very special* thanks to them! I am also indebted to Marilyn Laatsch for her editorial assistance in the final writing of this book.

Thanks also to Edward T. Hall, who stimulated my initial involvement in film analysis and also advised me on how to present the project report as a book, and to George and Louise Spindler for encouraging the writing of the final MS.

For editorial judgment as well as typing, I am most grateful to Lorraine de la Fuente and her staff of the Social Science Manuscript Service of San Francisco State College, who saw the work through in its earlier form as a report to the U.S. Office of Education; and to Irene Dea Collier and Mary E. T. Collier, who worked through its considerably expanded and repeatedly revised forms to make the present book.

Financial support for the fieldwork and the analysis came from the Institute for the Study of Man, the Wenner Gren Foundation, and the American Philosophical Society. Thanks to all these worthy organizations! Also to San Francisco State College, who kept my salary coming through a semester of research leave.

Contents

ALASKAN ESKIMO EDUCATION
*A Film Analysis of Cultural
Confrontation in the Schools*

The potential of an Eskimo future.

1 / Perspectives

THE CHALLENGE OF ESKIMO EDUCATION

Education for Indians and Eskimos is part of a century of effort to place them successfully in the mainstream of American life. The federal effort to educate Indians was a treaty obligation born out of the Indian wars and the Plains Indians' final defeat at the massacre of Wounded Knee. It seemed not unreasonable at that time to consider education as a terminal experience that would close the history of the Native American.[1]

But the Natives have not been assimilated, nor have they vanished. Rather, they have rapidly increased their number and are now a fast growing minority in the United States. Indians have demonstrated the need to be Indians, to be themselves, and even today this continues to be a perplexing problem in schools and acculturation in general. Too often education has resulted in conflicts demanding extreme personality change. For this reason, among others, Indian education has continued to be a negative experience.

Education for Native Americans is a controversial issue because—despite millions spent by federal, state, and public schools, and by the churches—Indian students too often appear less equal than ever before, as personal fulfillment becomes increasingly difficult in modern society. Generally schooling has *not* opened pathways to equal opportunity, psychologically or economically, for these culturally different students. Rather, the quality of their education has placed thousands of Native Americans on relief and many thousands more in the ghettos of cities—far too many. In a shocking way, the more they go to school, it seems, the less effective they become as human beings.

How should the White society educate the Red or Brown American? In search of an answer the U.S. Office of Education funded a National Study of American Indian Education, in an eleventh hour effort to salvage Native American education and to assist teachers in this task wherever Indians are in school. The film study of Eskimo schools was one unit of the National Study.

Under the direction of Robert J. Havighurst of the University of Chicago, the National Study conducted an extensive survey, with regional teams all over the

[1] The word "Indians" includes many distinct cultural groups; sometimes I will use it to include Eskimos as well, particularly when speaking of experiences all these groups share.

United States following the same program of testing instruments and scheduled interviewing.[2] Anthropologist and educator John Connelly, of San Francisco State College, was contracted as regional director for the Northwest Coast and Alaska. Connelly invited me to add a visual dimension to his evaluation by film research. It was hoped that this direct observational study would qualify the more abstract verbalized findings of the formal analysis.

The fieldwork was carried out in the spring of 1969, largely in the area of Bethel, an air hub and trading center on the Kuskokwim River in West Central Alaska. Here in the tundra along the winding waterways of the Kuskokwim the Eskimos live in many tiny fishing communities, each with its community elementary school operated by the Bureau of Indian Affairs. Near one village a Moravian Mission ran a children's home and their own eight-grade school. In Bethel itself the consolidated elementary and high schools were operated by the State of Alaska. While Connelly and his assistants, Ray and Carol Barnhardt, concentrated on the larger schools in Bethel, I began my film study in the remote river villages, then moved in to Bethel, and finally to the municipal public schools of Alaska's largest city, Anchorage—covering more than forty educational situations and collecting for analysis some twenty hours of classroom film data.

The purpose of the film study was to track the well-being of Eskimo children through all varieties of school environments of this region—mission schools, BIA schools, state schools, city public schools. In the following year the film data was systematically analyzed and evaluated by a team of four San Francisco State College students and graduates with training in both education and visual anthropology. A final report, combining their judgments, my own judgments, and my empirical field experience, was submitted to the U.S. Office of Education, and the bulk of this material has been incorporated into this book.

Perhaps I should have gone north with no preconceived ideas about Native education, but this was not the case with me nor with most of the members of the National Study teams. Though my knowledge of Eskimos was limited, I had experienced years of interaction with policies of the Bureau of Indian Affairs (BIA) and Indian education in other areas. Earlier fieldwork on the Navajo, and more recently a study of Indians relocated in the San Francisco Bay Area, had already raised in my mind serious questions about education for culturally different children. This certainly affected my research and directed my observations, indeed may even have weighted my view. Critically I was observing within an anthropological frame of reference and checking on many circumstances of education with which I was already familiar. Further, I had come north from eight years of seminar experience with college students working for teaching credentials, so I was bringing to my focus not only problems of Indian education but the challenge of American education in general. As I filmed, questioned, and listened, I was seeking answers for many problems and clarification for many dilemmas that have generally confounded education across cultures.

---

[2] Estelle Fuchs and Dr. Havighurst have just published a comprehensive report on the study, *To Live on This Earth: American Indian Education*, New York: Doubleday. Copies of regional reports and final reports presented to the U.S. Office of Education are available from ERIC (Educational Resources Information Center, Bureau of Research, U.S. Office of Education).

Also, I came north with the belief that there *is* success in Indian education, though it may be less easily defined than the more pervasive failure. I was seeking a fulfilling classroom where positive and additive learning took place. Such a model could offer teachers a foundation point for adapting learning for the culturally different. The first and basic question was: What developments might be needed in Indian education? I hoped some fine teachers would show me these needs. Beyond what teachers could demonstrate, I wanted to broaden the focus of the challenge *away* from conventional goals and standards *into* the emotional and cultural considerations which might lie far beyond the common expectation of what makes a school effective.

It is native to our American system to believe that success can be measured in monetary and technological accomplishment, and that dollar-rich budgets can relieve the basic problems of deprivation. An equally spontaneous approach has been to find villains and scapegoats. For years critics have pommeled what they considered "inferior" teachers and decried the material poverty of Indian schools. What if our study found the schools excellently equipped by contemporary standards and the teachers both dedicated and well trained? What if we found that the best equipped schools and teachers fared no better or worse than physically drab, ill-equipped schools with minimally trained teachers? What would we face then? We were alerted that the issue might not be the professionality of the education provided, but the *kind* of education and the *kind* of practices followed in teaching the emotionally and intellectually different Native child.

To appreciate how I filmed and what I observed in Eskimo schools, we should share together what I feel is the significant relationship between culture and learning, for this relationship *is* the major focus of this book. An important view I share with many colleagues is that there is a great difference between schooling and education. As Robert Roessel, first director of the culturally determined Rough Rock Demonstration School on the Navajo, puts it, "Education is everything that takes place in life." Schooling is a limited aspect of the learning experience. With this view, conceivably the larger and often the most important education takes place *before* school, continuously *outside* of school, and long *after* school. A powerful education can be obtained *with no school at all.* In a lifetime experience with Indians in the Southwest, I have been impressed by the acuteness and intellectual effectiveness of unschooled Pueblo and Navajo Indians, who often respond to complex modern legalistic challenges with more grasp than school-trained Indians. Does this suggest that Indian children can lose intelligence by going to schools? Or is it simply very difficult to use Indian intelligence in White programs? Throughout this study, total education rather than the interlude of schooling is the large concern. We want to know *how schooling affects education,* additively or subtractively. In the same reference we are concerned with how schools affect learning and the development of intelligence.

California schoolteachers frequently view their Indian students as unintelligent or retarded. This impression may have a basis of accuracy, for certainly many Indian students perform at a low level. The question the anthropologist must raise is: Do they enter school retarded, or do they become retarded through schooling? One of the casualties of acculturation, moving from one system of values to another, is that effective intelligence *can* be left behind.

An anthropological view of intelligence is that it is both learned and expressed within a cultural system. Ruth Benedict (1934) refers to this phenomenon as the "language of culture," through which man develops, communicates, and solves his life problems. The cultural language is the total communication of group-shared values, beliefs, and verbal and nonverbal language. *The intelligence of the Native child must be observed in this communication context.* Behavior outside one's own system can appear unintelligent. It is generally accepted that much of basic intelligence is formed in early childhood within a particular environmental program. Acuteness of mind rests within the first language, and the initial intelligence rests upon experiences in the first environment, whether that be desert, jungle, or Arctic snow. From this is born the resourcefulness and intellectual vigor that we hope will be the equipment of the child as he grows. This presents the dilemma that it may be difficult and sometimes impossible to utilize full intelligence except within the cultural system that nurtured the child. It is this challenge that presents crosscultural education as a conflict between cultures, deeply involving the personality and culture of both teachers and students.

In this perspective, effective education could be the degree of harmony between the students' culturally and environmentally acquired intelligence, and the learning opportunities and the intelligence-developing procedures and goals of the school. Reasonably, if significant conflict lies between Eskimo processes and the school, some variety of educational failure must be expected. Teachers may be seen teaching ideally *with* the flow of Native intelligence, or teaching negatively *against* the Native stream of consciousness. Granted, these are subtle energies, but they are there to be utilized or ignored, and they may well make the difference between a motivated or a "turned-off" classroom.

Western life style and technology have drastically altered the Eskimos' relation to the Arctic, as indeed they have altered indigenous life throughout the world. Realistically then, what should be the goals of schools in preparing Natives to survive in drastic and rapid change? Can schools offer needed new skills to cope with modern economic survival without weakening essential Native learning for success in the Arctic environment?

Because historically education for Native Americans was essentially the conflict waged to change the Indians into White men, I was prepared to see stress which often places the Native child in conflict with his own personality—stress resulting either from failure in mastering the school culture and hence failure in the teachers' eyes, or stress from success in mastering White style. Successful White education could become the double bind that leaves the child in a chasm between two worlds.

A significant question is: What is success in the eyes of the White educators? Relocation away from the village? Partial or complete rejection of Eskimo self? Are students often left in the traumatic confusion which may be associated with disorganized change? Workers in the field of Indian education have long been concerned over the high dropout rate among Indian students, and the later inability to cope with modern cultural and economic life. Other ethnic minorities, notably Spanish-American children, respond in similar ways to comparable circumstances. I was equally concerned about this confusion of personality which seemed to freeze effective development.

Do White teachers of Eskimos limit further the resources of their students by their attitudes toward the Eskimo life style? White people in Alaska are heard to say, "The villages have lost their economic function. There is no future for a bright well-educated Eskimo boy in the villages." Is the intelligence of the child locked significantly into the vitality of his village and the Arctic life style, so that if we condemn the villages, we are also rejecting the emotional well-being of the child, in school and out? In this light, is White education a support or an assault upon Eskimo vitality? Can we consider well-being in education without considering the solidarity of Eskimo life in the Arctic? Is there no place for Eskimo culture in modern survival education? Where and how could Eskimo skills be incorporated into the schools?

White education on the Navajo Reservation, whether missionary or BIA, has in the past consistently rejected Navajo-ness from the schools, as if to say, "Hang your culture outside, and take a shower before you come to class!" Even today the first step in a BIA kindergarten school on the Navajo is to strip the clothes off the youngsters and soap them down before they are *allowed* in the classroom. However hygenic this may sound, and however economically practical the White teachers' dim view of the Eskimo village may be, both reject symbolically and conceptually the Native children from the White education in the school. Let us be very clear: I am not talking about any single kind of school—missionary, BIA, state, or public. We are simply discussing and observing what is happening to Native children in *White* schools. Ironically, comparable rejections affect many White children, as well as other ethnic minorities in American education.

Traveling north my plane left Seattle and flew over four hours of snowbound wilderness. Surely the far Arctic is the outpost of the American continent. Here we could observe again the historic contact of modern White culture with ancient people, the Eskimos. The wilderness was vast beyond any of my conceptions. Schools were dots on the tundra; villages, clustered dots by frozen rivers or coastlines. But when I entered the village classrooms, I sensed that I had not traveled far. Here was the familiar conflict, the distance that frequently isolates teacher from students. I was immediately impressed that there were aspects of the Eskimo classroom that were shared with the inner-city schools or the Spanish-American schools in the Southwest. In greater dimension, I sensed I was witnessing the conflict involved in the westernization of ancient societies, or of affluent American education's attempts to communicate with and ideally to "uplift" students from poverty's community. The Eskimo world has been called the ghetto of the north, or in the words of Edward Kennedy as reported in the Anchorage press, "the Appalachia of the Arctic." How pervasive is this view? Are teachers able to break away from this ethnocentricity and educate Eskimos *as Eskimos*?

Intrinsically this book is a report of "White Studies" for Brown students, and the hardships and frustrations of administering such a curriculum laid down by culture-bound White values. I approached the Eskimo world as an isolated microcosm where the familiar circumstance of the crosscultural dilemma might be observed and its simplicity might offer fresh insights that would be useful to the Hong Kong Chinese immigrants in San Francisco as well as to the Eskimos and the American Indians.

Our queries may appear to go beyond the scope of our film data of Eskimo classrooms. Factually stated, they certainly do. But the drama in these classrooms goes far beyond the teachers' fulfillment of their professional roles. To give justice to the efforts and the generosities of these men and women, I feel the real challenge of their assignments must be appreciated. Positive education for Native Americans has baffled educators for decades. Brilliant schemes have been introduced and millions of dollars spent, with small return. I approached my Eskimo classrooms with this perspective, and all that has been written is toward appreciating the scope of the challenge. The landscape of education I am trying to describe is particularly critical for Eskimo and Indian students, but the dilemma is shared with all children who are different—Red, Brown, Yellow, Black, or White. Basically the challenge is the right to be one's own self, whether this be the personality of a single individual, or the collective personality of a group. I move forward in this writing, as I did in the field experience itself, seeking an educational definition that offers people, no matter how different from others, a productive place in the modern world. I write with conviction that not only are people and peoples inherently unique but that civilization is enriched and tempered by this diversified vitality. I see Native education (and there are Natives everywhere among us) as utilizing multitudes of cultural energies without which a free and equal world may never be formed. The pages to come describe the varied effort of many teachers to deal with this challenge. The descriptions of classrooms will share with you questions that remain unresolved: Why are we educating Eskimo students? Why do well-trained teachers so often choose to teach in the lonely school posts of Eskimo villages? And if Eskimos were genuinely offered equal educational opportunity, what would be the content of this experience?

FLIGHT THROUGH TIME AND SPACE

My winter departure from civilization and modernity of the "Lower Forty-Eight" was from Seattle-Tacoma International Airport. Flight northward was toward the Arctic frontier where symbolically man's survival still is within the grip of nature. Flight into the Arctic winter dusk from Juneau to Anchorage is surely over nature's domain—no track of road, no human sign, hour after hour of tundra land, icebound shorelines, and treeless mountain ranges. But this expanse, north to the Arctic Ocean, is the home of 53,000 Eskimos, Indians, and Aleuts, scattered over a half million square miles of tundra and forestland. It was hard to conceive of modern enterprise emerging out of this wilderness. It was hard to imagine man's living at all in such bleakness!

But in a few minutes I would be arriving at the city of Anchorage. Mountains suddenly leveled, and in the distance was an impossible blaze of lights—the city. The lights fanned out in a maze of brilliance. Ahead were the homes of 40,000 White men and an estimated 5,000 Native Alaskans. The plane was lowering fast. The wilderness was scattered. Blinking neon signs, red and blue, and ribbons of car headlights illuminated tall buildings and windows of tiny homes. Suddenly the wilderness that had been majestic and timeless seemed fragile. Only a few decades ago Anchorage had been a railroad construction camp. Now Anchorage was any small American city that had grown too fast. Gaudy bars, secondhand car lots, and glass-encased, self-consciously modern buildings, with piles of dirty snow. Sharply dressed men, girls in miniskirts despite the cold, American construction men in boots, fur caps, and cowboy hats. Here and there a Native—Eskimo women picking their way with care in sealskin *mukluks,* quiet Indian faces drifting along, bright eyes of a few Native children, oblivious to the modern pace and mechanization. Here was a model of what American know-how could do with the Arctic wilderness. As in any American city, cars streamed by, grinding the winter into black asphalt. Multitudes came in by plane, but as many more came in cars from California and Oklahoma—campers, trailers, wagons, sport cars. The wilderness was broken by the Alaskan Highway and by the constant air streams flowing to and from the "Lower Forty-Eight," Europe, and Japan.

My second journey through time was from Anchorage to Bethel, a western trading center on the second largest river in Alaska, the Kuskokwim, which flows from the mountainous interior to the Bering Sea. The city of Bethel—would it be ablaze like Anchorage? Wien Consolidated Airlines canceled the morning flight: snow. Nature had intruded!

The flight to Bethel was into an Arctic wind and flurries of snow. The plane interior was shabby with use. Freight was lashed down where passenger seats had been. An all-Eskimo detachment of National Guardsmen climbed aboard, on their way home to villages after a training period near Anchorage. They were heavily dressed in snow packs, army parkas, and ear-flap caps. They filled the plane with gentle laughter and pressed their noses against the windows as we angled upward in a deafening burst of jet engines.

We circled for altitude, leveled westward as Anchorage began shrinking, and finally disappeared in the grandeur of desolate white peaks. The wilderness closed beneath me again. No trails, no sight of man. For the next two hours it was incomprehensible that we would see man again; but we would, the miracle would happen, and out of nowhere would come the small city of Behtel.

When our plane crossed the peaks of the Kilbuck Range, a hundred miles inland from the sea, we were over the tundra lands of the Kuskokwim. As we descended to land at Bethel, we came in low over the river that meandered west in tortuous coils between dark shorelines of willow and spruce. There were trails of men here! Lines of sled and Sno-Go (snowmobile) trails up and down the frozen river to villages near and very far, located on the river banks or on equally coiled river tributaries. Here the river Eskimos have thrived with a precarious balance of fish, berries, rabbits, ducks, caribou, moose, bear, and an occasional seal swimming from the sea. The Eskimo villages were here when the first White man came two centuries ago. How much longer will they remain? Along with our Eskimo passengers were Army officers and city-dressed men with galoshes, overcoats and attaché cases. Why do they come? What schemes are in their heads? The very vacuum of the wilderness seems to draw White men into the Arctic, each a messenger, like myself, from the modern world.

After experiencing Anchorage, the emptiness of the Arctic seemed deceptive. How rapidly it was overrun in three years in the Gold Rush! And now oil, minerals, and civil and military aeronautics. The air highway to Europe leads over the North Pole. And every square mile of the wilderness is contended for as a potential sportsman's paradise, which covets every salmon, polar bear, and moose.

Modern men change nature and, of course, the lives of the Native people. Change them into what?

Wing flaps down for landing. Sno-Go and sled tracks below us converged on the straggled river front settlement of Bethel, a scattered mass of black buildings sending up plumes of steam. Bethel was not like Anchorage *yet.*

Bethel is principally an airport center for western Alaska, a defense base left from World War II, still with the helterskelter look of a habitation of hastily thrown-up buildings and Quonset huts. Bethel is an Eskimo city, for Bethel is the hub of a score of Eskimo villages located 5 to 80 miles east and west along the Kuskokwim waterways. But Bethel is also a bridgehead of modernity in the tundra. I felt I had stepped back in history, for Anchorage was such a bridgehead for White enterprise fifty years ago. But nature still holds Bethel in her grip! No water system, no sewage. Water is purchased by the barrel, and human waste removed by the bucketful. In the schools in Anchorage 7 percent of the students are Natives, but here in Bethel the consolidated elementary and high schools are dominated by an 85-percent Eskimo student body. Bethel *is* an Eskimo city. Would the White invasion tip the balance of this culture? Soon?

Bethel is an island in the tundra with barely twenty miles of roads. But cars moved grotesquely through its streets, past Eskimos on snowmobiles and masses of Natives and Whites walking over frozen roads to and from the Post Office, the state liquor store, and three major trading posts that straggled along the river. Below river pilings teams of sled dogs were tethered, wailing and barking while the Eskimo owners traded or just visited in the metropolis. Icy winds blew up and down the river or across the desolate tundra, driving against long squirrel and muskrat skin parkas of the Eskimo women, or against the surplus Air Force high-altitude clothing popular with so many Eskimo men.

My third journey back in time was from Bethel to the isolated village of Tuluksak that lay eighty miles eastward up river on a tributary of the Kuskokwim. Seattle to Anchorage to Bethel and now to journey's end, Tuluksak. Air wings had become smaller, a single-engine bush plane, equipped with skis and loaded with parcels and freight. Village landings would be on river ice. We gained very little altitude and flew eastward across the loops and bends of the Kuskokwim River, following, as it were, the multitude of sled trails with now and then the tiny shapes of a dog team coming or going from Bethel. Twenty minutes later the plane dropped down even closer. Tuluksak lay ahead, pointed out by the pilot. Tuluksak is a village of the tundra, another dot on the map of Alaska, a black design of tiny dwellings, where one hundred and fifty Eskimos, one White VISTA worker, and two White teachers survived together through the winter isolation.

The plane settled down for a ski landing on the river ice. Log and frame dwellings flashed by, the bright buildings of the Bureau of Indian Affairs school, the steeple of the Moravian church. Dark winter-clad villagers descended the snow banks of the river to the metal bird that links the village to the world. Mail, relief checks, newspapers, a hundred pounds of dog food. And I, the stranger, descended to the river ice; another White man had arrived. Eskimo children helped me with my gear, and I entered the village world amid wild barking of staked-out sled dogs.

Journey's end was this village along a small frozen river. There was a tiny Native store, an even smaller post office, a white and green painted Moravian church, and

The village of Kwethluk, twice the size of Tuluksak, has electric lights, a brightly painted BIA school, a Moravian church, and a Russian Orthodox church.

clusters of log and frame houses that loosely formed a village square or fronted on meandering pathways leading along the high river banks. Aside from the barking sled dogs it was very quiet. A few figures emerged, disappeared, or reentered dwellings. A village asleep in the Arctic half light. Further beyond lay the BIA school compound, discrete from the tiny log houses of the village.

Why had I come? Why had the lone young man VISTA worker come? Why had the BIA teachers, man and wife, come and remained teaching in the Arctic for twenty years? White teachers first came to the Kuskokwim to change Eskimos into Christians. I came to observe how White education affects the Eskimos. But we all came, in our separate ways, because we considered the Eskimos in deprivation. The missionary teachers came because they believed the Eskimos had no concept of the soul. The BIA had sent teachers because they found the Eskimos unhygienic and inept in mastering White ways. The VISTA worker came because he believed the village low in modern skills and community enterprise. I also came over anxiety about skills—skills either not taught in the White school or blocked by the White school by interfering with Native survival learning of how to live in the Arctic ecology. My concern was whether education was helping Eskimos live in the real world *as Eskimos*. But as an observer and an evaluator, I came as a White man like a hundred others who at one time or another have descended on this tiny dot of a village called Tuluksak.

How far back in time was this village? At what point in Eskimo destiny was White education attempting to meet the village's need? Here my study of Eskimo education began—in the most remote village in a two-teacher school in a community reputedly involved in the subsistance survival of the Arctic. I was dropping in from the skies into two centuries of aboriginal–White contact culminating in Eskimo survival today. Within this history was the BIA school, built close on the edge of Tuluksak.

I was impressed with the human warmth and skill of the BIA teachers when I entered the Tuluksak classroom. The first-, second-, third-, and fourth-grade classroom was a very cheerful room decorated with bright prints of farm animals and cutouts of paper flowers. The room was wonderfully clean and orderly; the children, cheerful and well-behaved if a bit sleepy. The teacher moved about the room, gently prodding or encouraging, speaking in a clear and friendly voice. The school was exceptionally well-equipped for a rural village of a 150 people. There were bright toys, White dolls, modern trucks, and a full library of children's books. I remembered seeing equally well-equipped new schools on the Navajo Reservation, where I had also worked with some very dedicated teachers.

For many reasons this well-run school was a baffling place to begin observing educational processes that were, in many eyes, failing the needs of Native students. The teachers, living in their well-run home in the same building as the classrooms, were skilled in their style of life, but even on first contact appeared far removed from the lifeway of even the most modern Eskimos of this remote village. All that I could note down from this first visit was that the school compound was a confrontation with Eskimo life. Was there anything wrong with this? Isn't education generally a confrontation? Certainly I would have been bewildered if this mature couple were trying to live like Eskimos. Instead these teachers were sincerely being themselves and living the properly fed and housed White style that suited their personality and background.

Two years and several months later I still feel evaluating Tuluksak baffling on an immediate classroom teacher-to-student relationship. It is difficult to write about this school without first considering the total context of the White confrontation with the Eskimo. To evaluate education for Eskimos, I find I must consider the total history and drive of White intruders, which include myself, and more than two centuries of Western influence on Native life. We must weigh the actualities that have been imposed on Native survival over the centuries of White contact. If we can do this we might conceive of a modern Eskimo and the world in which he could survive now. A distortion of the educational dilemma could occur when we lose this whole view. What the teachers were giving their students in Tuluksak was *real*, but maybe only one part of the *real* that Eskimos need to survive *now*. Before traveling further we should pause to look at the history and the emerging ethnography of the Kuskokwim Eskimos, or we may be unable to see the many silent dimensions of this well-run White school.

2 / Eskimos and White men on the Kuskokwim

ESKIMOS AND THE RUSSIAN FUR TRADERS

My search into the history of the Kuskokwim River Eskimos has been directed toward understanding the continuity that is so essential to the development of any people. In this approach of ethnography and history I share the view that education *is* a continuing process—out of the past, through the present and into the future. Hence lifeways and sequences of acculturation seem the place to start in considering education for the Native American.

The nature of White contact with Eskimos, or other Native people, holds important clues to education and acculturation. School is a major acculturative experience where Native children, or any children, learn to adjust and cope with the imposing world. For Eskimos, or Indians, Afro-Americans or Puerto Ricans, wherever an ethnic minority confronts a significantly different majority, this movement away from ethnic self is an experience that either can give essential cultural perspective or can assimilate the child into ineffectual oblivion. Blindness to Native history and insensitivity to Native self cut a deep chasm between the White teacher and his Eskimo students, a space that education too often fails to cross. This account of White–Eskimo relationships, past and present, is a description of this gulf that for two centuries has separated White men from Eskimos.

I am concerned specifically with the Eskimos living on the waterways of the Kuskokwim River in West Central Alaska. The material is based on my experiences on the Kuskokwim in the spring of 1969 and on four books that represent source accounts of this isolated Eskimo environment. Early history has been drawn from *Lieutenant Zagoskin's Travels in Russian America, 1842–1844* and from Wendell H. Oswalt's analysis of the chronicles of the Moravians in the region, *Mission of Change in Alaska,* supplemented by a missionary's personal account, Anna B. Schwalbe's *Dayspring on the Kuskokwim.* For contemporary ethnography I have drawn from Oswalt's *Napaskiak: An Alaskan Eskimo Community,* a detailed study of a Kuskokwim village distinctly comparable to those in which I worked. This range of observation—Russian trader, Moravian missionaries, a modern ethnographer, and finally the contemporary state, mission, and BIA school personnel with whom I talked—gives us a view of Eskimos as seen through White eyes.

Prehistory of the Kuskokwim is barely known, though archeological surveys show contemporary villages were lived in before the first exploring White men. For hundreds of years Yuk-speaking Eskimo have lived in the tundra of the Kuskokwim Basin, fishing for salmon, gathering berries, hunting moose, bear, deer, and small game for food, sharing both dialect and culture with the Eskimos in the southern reaches of the Yukon. Both groups are surprisingly similar to the traditional maritime Eskimos living northward along the Bering Sea. Though the Yuk dialect would not be understood in Kotzebue and Nome, the music, drumming, and dancing are essentially the same. Despite centuries in the Alaskan interior, the Kuskokwim people are still ocean-oriented, with a strong relation to the sea a hundred miles westward. Seal oil and meat are still the "soul foods," and *mukluks* are made from seal and walrus skins. Until a decade ago they hunted from traditional walrus skin kayaks, and two decades ago they lived in sod houses similar to dwellings still used along the coast. Their courage, laughter, and philosophy—and their tenacious skill with outboard motors and snowmobiles—are typically Eskimo.

Travelers, explorers, and more recently anthropologists have consistently admired the resourcefulness and survival intelligence of the Eskimos. Their uniqueness built no great architecture; for most traditional Eskimo housing, as seen in White men's eyes, appeared temporary. Building materials were scarce on the coast and tundra. Though life was migratory in the search for food, with dispersed hunting camps as well as villages, the character of life was social. The wealth of the Eskimo cannot be found in material culture; rather the richness was represented by courageous and skilled performance, intense self-respect and self-determination. Accounts of Eskimo culture throughout the Arctic all tell of severe limitations of life that we today call extreme deprivation. Out of severe limitation and struggle for survival the Eskimo personality was cast and a ceremonial culture was created.

The peoples of the world have always faced ecological challenges of survival—heat, cold, extremes of moisture and aridity. Out of such circumstances were created lifeways of hunting, gathering, fishing, or farming. Values of competition and cooperation, patterns of families and communities, and political, moral, and religious systems were created. When all these climes and circumstances are viewed, it is not clear that men form similar attitudes in response to similar environments. Writers like Ruth Benedict in dealing with personality point out that culture is also arbitrary, a result of choices of how to deal with environmental circumstances. Thus, the Athabascan Indians a hundred miles further inland faced an environment similar to that of the river Eskimos, but these two peoples have very distinct life styles and attitudes. The Kuskokwim people from earliest description have sustained a communal village style of culture. They could have broken down into extended family groups and lived in smaller bands as did the Athabascans, but they chose to be together. From the earliest observation their life has been village-centered, social, and family-involved. This characteristic is as true today as it was 150 years ago.

What was it like on the Kuskokwim in the 1840s? And what is it like today? How has White judgment of Eskimo life changed in the intervening 130 years? The observations of Lieutenant Zagoskin give us a baseline from which to work forward (Michael 1967).

Zagoskin observed that the Eskimos chose a social structure with maximum equality and minimal authority. Though they may have appeared as "children" in Western eyes, they were recognized as considerate with a highly socialized sense of individual well-being. Interpersonal concern was cited many times in Zagoskin's writings. Overt criticism or ordering other people to do service was avoided. Oswalt observed instances of this nature in the 1950s. So, in the face of extreme circumstances of limitation and sometimes starvation, the Kuskokwim people built a culture of remarkable sensitivity. Among other "primitive" people who are credited with a high degree of interpersonal refinement, we are reminded of Theodora Kroeber's story of Ishi, and of John Marshall's films and Elizabeth Marshall Thomas's writings on the Kalahari Bushmen.

The center of all ceremony, communication, and general education in the old days was the *kashgee* or *kazhim*, a spacious earth-covered structure which was the men's communal house.[1] Describing a twenty-four-day period in an Eskimo community, Zagoskin starts and finishes his account in this central dwelling. The *kashgee* could be compared to the Southwest *kiva*, where in archeological times a whole pueblo might gather for special ceremony (for example, the Great Kiva in the ruins at Aztec, New Mexico). In some villages the *kashgee* could accommodate 500 people, indeed all the villagers and guests from other communities.

This focal point of sociability and ceremony was also a ceremonial bathhouse for the men. Cleanliness may have been a basic purpose, but more, the bath was a time for men to socialize and to test their endurance for places of prestige. As if in balance with enduring bitter cold, the *kashgee* was a place to bear unendurable heat. Men of the village gathered round a snapping sprucewood bonfire with choking smoke that filled the *kashgee* before finding its way out the smoke hole. The room had tiers of benches, and while adolescents crouched on the floor, the strongest men suffered the heat from the highest tier where the smoke and heat were intense. Wads of shredded wood would be held to the mouth to filter out the smoke, and the endurance bath would proceed till, one by one, the men would crawl out or be carried out into the snow.

The *kashgee* was chiefly a dwelling place for men and boys, and here the mystique of the culture was passed on. Here travelers from afar were given lodging, food, and entertainment. Home was described as elsewhere, in other smaller earth-covered dwellings. Men might bathe, visit, and doze till past midnight, and then slip away to join their wives or keep clandestine rendezvous. The organizing process of the *kashgee* continued up to the proselytizing of the Moravians, which succeeded finally in undermining its function forever.

Russian enterprise had begun in the Aleutians and Kodiak Island in 1741. In the following century Russia established the fur trade in Alaska and finally as far south as California. The first Russian explorers, fur traders and imperialists, were familiar with the steppes and forested wilderness of Siberia where standards of life were not so different from those of the Eskimos. For sheer survival the Russians had to accept many Eskimo standards, foods, and technology, or perish.

There is little account of Russian women in the early decades in Alaska, and there was a generous intermingling and marriage with Native women. By the time the Russian American Fur Company penetrated the Kuskokwim in the early 1800s,

---

[1] *Kashgee* is the form preferred by Oswalt for the men's house. Michael, in a comparative vocabulary, gives *kazhim* as the Russian word and *kazhzhyyak* as the form in the Kuskokwim dialect. The early Moravians called it *kashima*, while Mrs. Schwable used the term *kashige*. Anderson and Eells spell it *khashgii*.

a large part of the company personnel was "Creole," which in the Alaskan context means Russian mixed with Aleut, Indian, or Eskimo. The most successful manager was himself a Creole. Thus, relations with the Eskimos in this period were far more relaxed for the Russians than for the Moravian missionaries who came later.

The Russian traveler, Lieutenant Lavrentiy Alekseyevich Zagoskin, who came to the Yukon and Kuskokwim on a tour of inspection in 1842, found the Kuskokwim Eskimos living on the edge of hunger and sometimes starving, so severe were the long winters. Leaving marine hunting grounds, where some sea mammals are available year round, may have posed subsistence problems for the river Eskimos. They had come inland because of stable salmon fishing and had learned to exist on fish. But salmon fishing techniques were not so efficient as today. And what happened if the fishing harvest had been small, or if for some reason a cache were destroyed, or if spring were too long in coming? The vast tundra offered little other food that could support a sedentary population. Large animals, moose, bear, and caribou could not be depended upon; they ranged too widely. Caribou herds moved fast and could disappear in the night, and the river Eskimos lacked the technology for inland hunting in winter. Through the long winters and into the spring when fish supplies ran low, there was hunger in the river communities. The winter solstice ceremonies of many northern peoples describe the hardships of winter hunger. So often the legend is the same, whether this be the premedieval Santa Lucia ceremony of Sweden or the winter solstice deer dance of the Pueblo Indians. The village is starving, the snow too deep for hunting, stored foods have run low. Then a miracle saves families from starvation. In Sweden it is a Viking ship coming across the waters loaded with food. In Taos Indian pueblo in New Mexico it is the charming of the deer by two deer mothers who lure the game to the village.

Much of Zagoskin's account is of mutually shared hardship. The Russian post and the Eskimo villagers together had difficulty surviving on the limited game in the area, particularly through the last terrible weeks of winter, when dried fish supplies were depleted and travel to hunt for game became ever more perilous as spring approached and the river ice grew more rotten. Even today a delayed spring is a lean time as stores run low. The Kuskokwim posts were marginal operations, with only limited support from the Russian American Fur Company whose head-quarters were far off at the mouth of the Yukon. Russian traders and Eskimos alike had to exist on occasional birds, rabbits, or other small game, though the Russians with guns could apparently hunt game that the Eskimos were unable to bring down either with snares or bow and arrows. Zagoskin's journal describes these days:

April 17th. Murky; occasionally fine snow; a fresh north by northeast wind until noon; in the evening a south by southeast wind with light rain squalls.
   In the evening one of the returning hunters delighted us. He and the Tungus [shamans] had succeeded in shooting two deer and in capturing three bear cubs; the she-bear had run away. It is strange that she decided to leave the cubs. The tundra is almost entirely clear of snow. The dogs are exhausted and the loaded sled is stuck in an overflowing draw about 3 miles from the fort. The hunter has come for help. Who would refuse a piece of good meat!

April 18. Murky and a fine snow in the morning; a gentle west wind. Slightly cloudy in the afternoon, gentle north by northeast wind.

Of the 5 *puds* [*pud,* a Russian measure weighing 36.11 pounds] and 35 pounds of deer meat, the men at the fort were given 2 *puds* and 12 pounds. Thus it came about that we helped those who were supposed to help us; praise God, but without a reliable weapon I would have not agreed to survey the Kuskokwim . . .

In place of fresh fish, which has not been caught since the 16th, the natives are cooking dressed sealskin and the bladders, which are empty of fat. Occasionally someone gets a grouse, someone else a duck, the lucky ones a goose. All of this food is given to the children (Michael 1967:257).

There are accounts of Russian ruthlessness and insensitivity to the Natives and their ecology. There are stories of cruelty and massacres of Natives in the Aleutians. But by the time the Russian American Fur Company penetrated the Kuskokwim, the great wilderness and the need of collaboration with Indians and Eskimos greatly modified their behavior. Their dealings with the Kuskokwim Eskimos were inept but friendly. As stated, they "starved together" when hunger stalked the river. The accompanying Orthodox priests were generally benign and made little inroads on the ethnic well-being of the Eskimos. Lieutenant Zagoskin, representing the Czar and the Russian American Fur Company, laid down in his report what might be considered the guidelines of protocol between the traders and the Eskimos.

In conclusion let me repeat that whether our trade flourishes or diminishes in this region depends enormously on the ability and good intentions of the man in charge of the post. The native is very appreciative of kind treatment. He sometimes finds himself in need of certain things for which he is unable to pay, but no credit is extended. But if the man in charge handles his affairs in this way, the take in furs will not cover his expenses. Similarly his profit will be small if he plays the gentleman, as is done, for example, at Fort St. Michael, and does not allow anyone in his room. Lukin has always kept open house; we have often seen a dozen natives in his little room who will wait silently for days at a time until he returns from his work in the woods or at the fish-trap. If guests arrive at meal-time, the piece of *yukola* [dried fish] and the teapot of "colonial" tea are divided among those present. As he knows their customs well, he never asks who a visitor is or for what purpose he has come (Michael 1967:255).

The protocol of the Russian American Fur Company was considerably more formal, but also reflected the human necessity for genuine collaboration with the Eskimos. The very survival of their enterprise depended upon this. Zagoskin reports in his journal the company's instructions to Lukin, manager of the post on the Kuskokwim:

In the four villages nearest to the Khulitna, as I have designated, inform my friends and acquaintances that I wish them to be *toyons* [tribal elders, term brought from Siberia; elders from each village who were appointed overseers by Russian American Fur Company were called *toyon.*] (Michael 1967:332) in those villages, and to have honor and fame from God and our beloved Commander-in-Chief. I beg you to receive them as trusted friends, diligent in the interests of the Company, with their loyal relations and close comrades, and to procure medals for them, and for them to be loyal subjects of our tsar Nicholas Pavlovich (Michael 1967:285).

From the first contact in the 1700s the Russians were involved in educating Native Americans. The White man with his superior sophistication readily assumes the role of teacher to the Native. Zagoskin was no exception, and he made some significant observations on the educational effect of removing Natives from their environment to a role in the larger Russian posts. Zagoskin observed that Creoles growing up in the relatively civilized atmosphere of the posts were not as effective as those living in the bush.

> One has to admit that in practical experience all Creoles living in the outlying division far surpass their fellows who have grown up in the principal settlements of our colonies. This is only natural. From the time he is small, the Creole in the hinterland is trained to work and by his native keenness of wit and alertness he develops into a bold hunter who is resourceful in the emergencies that frequently arise (Michael 1967:262).

This observation refers to the Creole, but with Native Eskimos the principle remains the same. Zagoskin complained that Native girls who married into the settlements learned to dance European steps and adjusted to a life of relative leisure, but they gave up their Native skills and ability to work. The ineptness of Native girls gone civilized in the Russian settlements was so disturbing that in 1837 a women's training school was founded under the auspices of the wife of the commander-in-chief of the colonies. The goal of the school was "to provide well-brought-up and industrious housewives for the growing generation of Creoles," who must have represented the expanding population of Russian America. Zagoskin observed,

> At present each pupil learns to sew and to dress birdskins and to make rain-parkas, to weave various household articles such as mats and others of grass and various roots—all things highly useful to women who intend sharing their husband's work in their homeland (Michael 1967:301).

This is a far cry from a Home Economics class today in Bethel High School. In 1837 the Russians were willing to skip European academics and elegance for education to live in the Arctic ecology.

Zagoskin as a White teacher was critical of the educational attitude of some of his Russian colleagues. Commenting on company employees who exploited the credulity of the Eskimos to represent advanced technology as magic, Zagoskin says:

> In showing them my watch, the compass needle, the force of gunpowder, etc., I tried as much as possible to acquaint the native with the structure and use of these objects. I explained to them that this is all the result of the cleverness of man, and that they too, if they wished, could learn to do likewise (Michael 1967:108, 292).

Zagoskin also observed some of the pathos of the shift from subsistence to trapping for trade goods after watching Upper Kuskokwim Eskimos trade within an hour 164 beaver pelts, 4 otter, 2 deer, and 2 black bear skins for a handful of trinkets.

> Each one covered his head with a blue cloth cap with red piping, and laid in a year's supply of tobacco, beads, flint, and sealskin thongs for taking deer. . . . The carefree children of the North dressed themselves up and started to dance.

> We must recall that a beaver pelt is of no value in the eyes of the native. He kills the beaver for its meat, but only uses the hide as a last resort to make socks, or thongs for deer nooses. We must remember that 10 years ago we

found this native with a stone ax, bone needles, in a cold beaver-skin parka, starting a fire by rubbing together two wooden sticks, and without any practical domestic utensils. We must not judge too harshly the fact that he sometimes exchanges what is of no use to himself for something which has little in our eyes. The northern native needs education as does a child; his education depends on us. At the present time his prosperity on earth depends on the possession of a gun and 10 rows of potatoes. This could be achieved with comparative ease (Michael 1967:269–270).[2]

Here White education began. What did the Eskimo need then for survival, and what does the Eskimo need now? Can we say today with any conviction that the problems and the solutions are appreciably different from those the Russian lieutenant analyzed 130 years ago?

The Russian influence, ending in 1867, appeared to have effected little change in Kuskokwim culture in terms of subsistence, technology, or hygiene. The stability of the Eskimo life style in this period is partly explained by the survival balance of fishing. The Russians introduced firearms, which broadened the survival base, and they introduced a trading economy based on currency in the form of beaver pelts. Certainly hunting beaver for trade, trapping for trade goods rather than for food, tipped the Eskimo's ecological relationships and drastically altered many associations. But apparently these did not disturb the balance of the fishing economy. Salmon was the reason for the Eskimo's presence on the Kuskokwim, and even today salmon remains the ecological hub of survival. This is in contrast to the experience of inland Eskimos in the Hudson Bay region who died away completely after the Hudson Bay Company lured them away from caribou hunting to trap for the company; then when the fur market collapsed, these Eskimos were technologically unable to return to caribou hunting, and in a short time the group perished.

The Russians were the Eskimos' first White teachers. Significantly they had made the Kuskokwim Eskimos aware of the surrounding White world with its exotic wares, concepts of improved living conditions, and an image of Christianity. The Russian priests taught the Natives the litany of the Russian Orthodox religion and some aspects of Christian morality. They were permissive teachers; the few demands they made on the Eskimos were essentially ceremonial—that they cross themselves, learn the chants, and attend to the ornate Orthodox calendar. In a real sense the Russian Orthodox missions turned ceremony over to the Eskimos, for so rarely were priests able to visit the villages. When the Russian empire withdrew Orthodoxy remained, mystically absorbed into Eskimo ceremony.

THE COMING OF THE MORAVIANS

The sale of Alaska to the United States only briefly interrupted the fur trade, since an American receiving company took over the crumbling assets of the Russian

---

[2] The Russians brought many new foods to Alaska including successful vegetable gardening. Today there are only meager gardens here and there in the villages. Yet agriculture still holds a promise for Arctic Alaska. Long summer days promote excellent growth and make up for the short season. In the 1930s the Farm Security Administration established a successful farming community near Anchorage, which today thrives commercially on vegetables and potatoes, milk and eggs.

American Fur Company. But it was almost two decades before a new and different American influence entered the area: missionaries from the Moravian Church, an Evangelical Protestant sect which had been founded in Bethelem, Pennsylvania, in the early eighteenth century and which had long been active in the mission field among American Indians.

Sheldon Jackson, a Presbyterian educator and reformer, first drew the attention of the Moravians to the Kuskokwim as a new field worthy of their zeal. Traveling in Alaska in the 1870s, Jackson became greatly concerned about conditions of Eskimo life, by poverty and squalor and what he considered moral degeneration, which he attributed to unwholesome White influences. He felt that the encroaching White culture had already destroyed the traditional Eskimo culture and broken down their economy, and that only a major effort of wholesome White influences, namely Christian missionaries, could save them from depravity. It was in direct response to his lectures in the United States that the Moravians decided to go to the Kuskokwim (Oswalt 1963a:16–17).

Yet when we compare Jackson's account to that of Zagoskin forty years earlier, it seems not unlikely that a large part of Jackson's reaction was one of extreme culture shock at many normal elements of Eskimo life style—a style that White sensibilities *still* find upsetting today. The poverty and squalor were reported in almost the same terms by Zagoskin. Hunger has always stalked man in the Arctic. Housing was primevally crowded, and practices of hygiene were (and still are) ecologically restricted.

The Moravian mission came to the Arctic a century later than the Russians. The westward movement of the United States had come much closer to Alaska in that century. Alaska was an extension of the American frontier and the vigorous expansion of western progress. The Moravians came as teachers from the United States of the 1880s, representing the good life of technology and material achievement. Despite early frontier hardships, the Moravians were to stay and bring modern White values to the Eskimos. It was a double drive, to bring not only Protestant Christianity but the material values, hygiene, and educational fulfillment of White America as well.

No doubt the missionaries carried in their mind's eye the orderly image of Bethlehem, Pennsylvania, the spiritual home of their denomination. What had been in the Russians' image? The vast wastes of Siberia? The primitive peasant communities everywhere in eighteenth-century Russia? There was far less discrepancy in conditions between Alaska and Russia than between Alaska and the eastern seaboard of the United States a century later. Reasonably the expectations of the Moravians were far different from those of the Russians, who were there to get fur and survive as best they could. The Moravians came as teachers and missionaries to bring "the good life" as well as "the good news" that the Eskimos could enter heaven and be freed from their pagan, poverty-stricken life; they saw it as their calling to endure their hardships until American modernity would come and ease their lot and bring further enlightenment to the river Eskimos.

As teachers they came as outlanders and predictably would return where they came from. The Eskimos had come in such a dim past that they believed they had always been there. The message of the missionaries and other White educators might be stated: "Yes, you have always been here in this dreadful place, but through our teachings you will be liberated to leave." It is creditable to the zeal of the Moravians that some of them did not leave but stayed on till death came by accident or old age. Nevertheless the Kuskokwim was a place to leave, because of the hardships, the isolation, the intense cold, the summer mosquitoes, and the often revolting life of the Natives, including their Christian converts. This revulsion was no particular fault of the missionaries. They were as a group generous and dedicated, but they were White with customs, values, and styles that made the aboriginal ways of Eskimos unacceptable and shocking. And of course, while many stayed on, others left within a couple of years for medical reasons, for culture shock, or for comfort in their retirement. So despite the continuous residence of many of the mission's founders, the pattern throughout the mission history was the same as today: to endure with self-sacrificing zeal, but eventually to go home again.

Epigramatically, the very ecology and life style that challenged missionary zeal also quietly became a measure of their fulfillment that ordered life in the states did not offer. Individually, I am sure, the Arctic and the Eskimo entered the missionaries' psyche, but their Christian programming appeared to keep these involvements out of their teaching. In appreciation of this problem, White teachers today on the Kuskokwim also get deeply involved in the Arctic drama, but as with the Moravians, the drama that lures White teachers to lonely Alaska today only rarely finds its way into the ordered White classrooms.

This brief writing cannot fathom the motivations of Christian missionaries, and members of the White race in general, that send us to the farthest corners of the world to sell our way of life. Humanly we seem to be searching for a challenge our home place does not offer, and many of us find our fulfillment as outlanders in strange places. The compulsion may be both aggression and, on the part of religious missionaries, guilt. Christianity is not the only creed of civilization, but historically Christianity has been territorial. By fire and sword the lands must be wrested from the colored infidels by the White crusaders. Dr. Albert Schweitzer, certainly one of the inspired Western missionaries, could not accept his precocious success as a young professor at the University of Strasbourg, saying, "It struck me as incomprehensible that I should be allowed to lead such a happy life, while I saw so many people around me wrestling with care and suffering" (Schweitzer 1949:84). He tried absolving his guilt in various ways and finally determined to practice medicine in the most difficult and primitive locale in the world, in search of his own salvation; at any rate, Lambarene deeply fulfilled Schweitzer's need.

Moravian teachers on the Kuskokwim today seem equally fulfilled, friendly, warm people. For the Moravians, of course, the challenge was to save Eskimo souls in the rigors of the Arctic. With exemplary ethnocentrism Christians are prone to feel that other peoples have no concept of the soul—indeed that the soul is lost except through Christian salvation. This suggests that they approach the Eskimo to be converted with the preconceived image of an empty vessel to be filled. The student in the classroom waiting to learn is perceived in the same way. Again, out of appreciation of the cultural stranger, it is questionable whether the White teachers in Alaskan schools today have an appreciably greater respect for cultural difference than did the early pioneer educators of the 1880s. What is this image that is so significant to the goals and content of White education for Eskimos or Native people most anywhere? We suspect the image is drawn with the same chalk whether teachers come to preach Christianity or simply to represent what they feel to be a superior society.

Moravian writings describe vividly their first reactions to the Eskimos. Hartmann and Weinland were the Moravians who first surveyed the Kuskokwim area in 1884 for a possible mission site. Oswalt summarizes their reports:

> They were appalled by what they saw. They regarded the living conditions as filthy beyond description, and the Eskimos were far more backward than they had anticipated. Two things, however, impressed them beyond all else: the mosquitoes and the lice (Oswalt 1963a:19).

After being in the field for nearly two years, Weinland was still very displeased with the Eskimo behavior:

> Taken as a class, the Yuutes are decidedly phlegmatic in temperament. They are content to take things as they come, be it threatened starvation or over-abundance, be it intense cold or drenching rain, all seem to be regarded as so many phases of life which must necessarily be experienced, & to try to alleviate which they hardly dream. Life is to them one prolonged series of sufferings; such as but few could endure, & yet suicide is unheard of among them. They are deeply rooted in their habits & manner of living, & it is a difficult matter to get them to adopt even the most striking & most evidently necessary changes. White men have been living in their midst for half a century, and yet today their mode of living is rude, uncivilized, filthy. Taken as a class, the Yuutes are dishonest, thievish, and their word cannot be trusted. In trade, they will rarely acknowledge that they are in debt, and it seems to be their highest ambition to defraud the traders. They cannot be called robbers, for they are too cowardly to steal any large articles. But pilfering of small articles under circumstances where detection is difficult, this is common, & to be found out appears to be a greater disgrace than the wrong doing itself (Oswalt 1963a:28).

This observation is a brilliant summing up of Native pragmatism on the one hand and the White man's ethnocentric concepts of morality on the other. Weinland reflects his feelings in detail in a letter describing the indigenous half-submerged sod house called a *barabarrah*, that is built with a tunneled entrance to keep out the cold:

> Through this tunnel I must crawl every time I go to see my two patients. . . . Emerging from the tunnel, through which you have squeezed past several dogs, groped in the darkness, and raised a curtain of dirty matting, you find yourself in the barabarrah, or house proper. It is about twelve feet square, with matting lying on the ground around the four sides. When I entered this evening, it was dark, and calling for lights, a sight was disclosed, which, alas, is but too common. In this small space, dirty, filthy, and filled with an indescribable stench, were *fifteen* persons, men women and children, besides several dogs. The space in the centre of the barabarrah is always occupied by buckets of water, dishes of food, slop pails, etc. (Oswalt 1963a:29).

I sympathize with Weinland's reactions. Indeed it was an extreme step from Pennsylvania to the conditions of the Kuskokwim. For most of us, Christian or not, thrown in this same circumstance, our reactions probably would be the same. Quite aside from moral considerations, White value judgments were then and still are very inflexible toward what we consider hygiene. Filth, overcrowding, stench, and darkness are bound to shock our sensibilities. The culture shock of the Moravians certainly must have blurred the Eskimo personality. Culture shock is blinding and negative and must have made it difficult for the missionary teachers to work with the positive elements of Eskimo life. The missionaries intended to save the Eskimo from his sufferings and despair, even though as Weinland was sensitive enough to note, the conditions he found shocking were of little importance to the Eskimos.

Missionary sentiment is expressed poetically in *The Moravian* published in June 1895 (Schwalbe 1951:29):

The Cry of the Alaskan Children

Far from the islands of Bering's dark sea
Comes the sad cry of the children to me,
Help, in the name of the Father of all;
Give to us, starving in body and soul.

Out of our misery gather us in,
Give us a refuge from suffering and sin.

Mrs. John Kilbuck, one of the original group of missionaries, wrote to a New Bedford paper defending the value of the mission work and inviting any doubters to come and see the results, saying, "It requires only about six months of proper Christian influence to change the listless animal-like expression into one of intelligence" (Schwalbe 1951:30). This speaks not only of the academic accomplishment of the mission school but also of the aptness of the Eskimo student to be able in only six months to communicate sensibly with his Christian teachers in ways that allowed them to appreciate that the Eskimos were indeed intelligent and capable of human feelings.

Anna Buxbaum Schwalbe, missionary from 1909 to 1948 and author of the Moravian chronicle *Dayspring on the Kuskokwim,* observed as did Weinland that the misery of the Eskimo was primarily in the eyes and hearts of the missionaries —which was a major problem in conversion.

In the earliest years high moral standards were entirely lacking. The people seemed to fail to see the enormity of it all, saying that such were their customs and that it had never marred their happiness. Little girls of nine or ten were made prostitutes by their parents. Polygamy was practiced. Women thought nothing of leaving their husbands and vice versa. Men travelling from village to village exchanged wives. Cruelty was common. Nothing was thought of the killing off of unwanted infants, especially girl babies. The missionaries knew of one old woman believed to be a witch or shaman who was said to have caused the death of several children. She was clubbed to death, her joints severed, and she was burned in oil. The dead were wrapped in skins or doubled up into a rude coffin. Sometimes they were placed on scaffolds out of the reach of dogs. More often they were placed on the tundra where they were devoured by the hungry beasts (Schwalbe 1951:30).

Most of these observations are ethnographically sound and similar instances noted by less partisan reporters. But the missionaries were unable to see the reasons and the functions of the manners and morals that so shocked them, nor had they the historical perspective to see an affinity between the witch incident described above and the pillorying, burning, and drowning of witches in their own not too distant European and New England Protestant background.

The Russian traders had to survive by ecological cooperation with the Eskimos. The early Moravian missionaries also had to master many of the Eskimos' skills and help one another through the long winters. On many levels life may have been even harder for them than for the Russians, for the Moravians came far less prepared to deal with Arctic life and Native values. But despite essential survival interaction with the Eskimos, cultural difference drew the curtain so completely over Eskimo personality that even when circumstance did present the humanism of the Eskimo, and the missionaries acknowledged these breakthroughs, still they were unable to incorporate these insights into their programming.

A number of missionary wives bore children in Bethel, and there was concern as to whether this was a good addition to the missionaries' work.

Of one mission family Mrs. Schwalbe writes:

"Christie," the eldest, ran in and out of the native cabins, speaking the Eskimo language, accepting their friendship and rejoicing greatly over the small boats and the bows and arrows that the old men carved for him and the little boots and other fur garments that the grateful mothers and grandmothers offered in token of their love for the small Cossayagak (little white boy). More often than not, although the mothers on the field view with the greatest concern the possibility of the contaminative influences, children have to be a very real blessing. "Now you are really one of us" is the expression frequently voiced by the native women when the first-born comes to the missionary mother (Schwalbe 1951:74).

We see that Eskimos love children after all and pay homage to the first born, which is in contradiction to earlier missionary observations on the callousness of Eskimo parents about children.

Equally significant, as Schwalbe (1951:87) notes, is the fact that "Christie," born on the Kuskokwim, in spite of his missionary parents, "ran in and out of the native cabins, speaking the Eskimo language, accepting their friendship. . . ." Apparently Eskimo domestic life that still shocks White teachers today did not bother Christie, even as a missionary child.

Death came to the missionary children too. In 1901 a whooping cough epidemic carried away many children, including the infant son of a missionary. The natives, full of sorrow and expressing their grief, came to the Weinlick home. It is at such times that one comes to realize fully the sympathetic heart of the Eskimo. Some have pronounced them an apathetic, stoical race of people. It may be that what seems to be a mask of indifference, merely covers a kind of timidity, a hesitancy to show a flood of emotion that once opened could not be controlled. Certain it is that the heart is overflowing with love. Death has been such a frequent visitor, that, schooling themselves against his coming, they have learned a calmness that few of us achieve. They do not say, "We shall die" but rather "We shall cease living," or "We shall go from this earth" (Schwalbe 1951:87).

This is an important observation about Eskimo compassion gathered from a circumstance that happened in the early decades of the Moravian mission. Reasonably this describes Eskimos prior to extensive Christian teaching. Unless we support the missionary thesis of nigh-instant personality change experienced by Christian conversion, I feel this early record of Eskimo sentiment offers a positive foundation for describing the Eskimo personality as it was before the Moravians opened their first boarding school in Bethel.

MORAVIAN INVOLVEMENT IN
THE LIFE ON THE ESKIMOS

The missionaries found the river Eskimos living in organized communities with a fulfilling ceremonial life expressed in the potlatches or giveaway ceremonies[3] and other communal activities surrounding the *kashgee*. As earlier described, this communal male dwelling was a center where the whole village could assemble. For the Eskimo man, day began and ended in the *kashgee*. It was the hub of all enterprise. For the boys it was also the school and the portal which led into manhood. The missionaries first witnessed the richness of Eskimo culture in the *kashgee*, and it was within the *kashgee* that the missionaries first preached their gospel. Weinland described a ceremony he and Kilbuck visited in Napaskiak in 1886, probably a "Boys Dance."

> On entering the kashima, we saw the men hard at work making masks, & finished masks standing around everywhere. We were greeted very cordially, different ones inviting us to their seats on the benches. . . . Before long four drums were brought in, & a practice of the real ekorushka was held. [*Ekorushka* is a Russian-derived term under which the Moravians lumped most of the Eskimo ceremonies.] A young man, masked, & holding a wood chip in each hand, took his seat on the floor of the kashima. A young man knelt opposite him, & back of this one, stood a woman & young girl. At a given time one of the drummers opened the performance by beating time on his drum, while the masked young man began some peculiar jirations, which were imitated by the young man opposite to him, & by the females standing further back. In a few minutes the other drums joined in, an old man dictated a song, & the entire company joined in singing. Following this came an interlude, during which the singing ceased, while the drumming & the corresponding jirations continued. Thus six parts were gone through with, the entire performance lasting about fifteen minutes. . . . The entire performance was not regarded as anything serious, for the more ridiculous it could be made the better it was liked . . . (Oswalt 1963a:59–60).

Two days later they returned for the actual ceremony. This had not yet begun when the missionaries arrived, but they were ushered into the men's house to wait.

> He told us to go to the kashima meanwhile, where we found some of the natives practicing their parts. A large number of masks were hung around the kashima, & my first thought when I entered the place was, "This looks like a fair." Four male performers, wearing large masks of most wonderful designs, and one female performer, occupied the stage, & were going through peculiar jirations, keeping time with the beating of eight drums, four on each side of the stage. Soon after our arrival an intermission was taken, during which the women & children filed out. This gave me an opportunity to count them, & I found that one hundred & twenty people had been in the kashima. . . .

> Near the roof of the kashima hung two representations of birds, the one of an eagle, the other of a sea-gull. On the eagle stood a stuffed representation of a male native & on the seagull that of a female. Upon inquiry I learned that these

---

[3] Oswalt refers to the giveaway ceremonies as "potlatches," saying this term is frequently used by Whites in describing the ancient communal ceremonies of the Kuskokwim Eskimos. The relationship between these ceremonies and the potlatches of the Northwest Coast Indians is very remote.

represented the spirits of deceased natives being borne upward after death. The kashima was cold and draughty, and, as I had wet feet, I began to feel very uncomfortable (Oswalt 1963a:60–61).

On first experience the missionaries did not equate religious experience with the *kashgee* performances because they looked "like a fair" and because "the more ridiculous it could be made the better it was liked." In their Protestant Christian eyes there could be no mixing of sacred and profane, of religious ceremony and entertainment, so they were unimpressed at any possible religious significance of the performance. It was not until later that the Moravians realized the true significance of the *kashgee* ceremonies.

A major function of many gatherings was the giving and receiving of gifts. The gift-giving ceremonies described by the Moravians appeared sincerely directed to sharing, despite any social recognition achieved by the host community and the gift-giving individuals.

> They play it in this way. They ask the presents of each other. First, the women asked for what presents they wanted of the men; then the men of the women. The women came together, got a long stick, tied strings to it at intervals of about an inch, then passed it around to each woman, who tied something, anything to the end of one of the strings and named what she wanted. The leader took particular note of what she said and the string she tied to. When all the women had asked for something the leaders took the stick to the men and told them what each string called for and whom it belonged to. Each man then took off one or more of the strings and got as nearly as he could what was asked for. When all have their presents ready they meet, and the women also come together. As soon as all have arrived at the place of meeting they begin to sing and dance and present their gifts, with a dish of something to eat along with it. If they are able they give more than was asked of them; if not, it is never noticed. When all is over, the men in like manner ask presents of the women (Oswalt 1963a:61).

Missionary accounts written in these early years continue to describe the splendour and generosity of the ceremonies. Considering how rude and distasteful the missionaries considered the physical level of Eskimo life, no doubt they were baffled and impressed by what they first considered to be merry entertainment to make life more tolerable for the Eskimos. Weinland, considering his first impressions of the kashima programs, made this observation.

> We are unanimous in the opinion that so far as these different performances themselves are concerned, there is nothing immoral in them, but that much immorality is carried on under cover. It cannot well be otherwise, where so many uncivilized people are herded together (promiscuously).[4]

Weinland and the succession of missionaries that followed him certainly expected to find scenes of primitive orgies, and they must have been surprised and relieved at finding lifeways among the Eskimos as well-ordered and civil as they were.

On first contact missionaries did not feel the Kuskokwim Eskimos had a religion, or if they had, it was being forgotten. Young people were unable to discuss the supernatural, and only under great pressure would the old people reveal that they

---

[4] Oswalt 1963a:67. The parenthetical "promiscuously" is Oswalt's interpretation, as is other parenthetical material in quotations from Moravian texts.

did indeed have a religious system. As in many indigenous societies, Eskimo religion was rightfully the domain of the elders and passed on to the people only by the old people. This circumstance could have misled the missionaries into believing that pagan beliefs were of little threat to Christianizing the Eskimo. Yet Weinland found evidence that the Eskimos had very complex beliefs about the soul, the supernatural, and life after death. Working through an interpreter, he recorded what he felt was the basis of Eskimo religion.

> They believed in both a good & an evil spirit. The good spirit was in the higher regions where the crow flies, & hence, they named him "Crow." They did not worship the crow itself as an image of that god, they did not pray to the good diety, nor did they sacrifice to him. They simply felt instinctively that there was a higher being who was creator & preserver of the world, & they taught their children "Do not do anything bad, for He sees you."
> The evil spirit existed, but they had no name for him, & do not seem to have concerned themselves any further about him.
> They believe that death does not put an end to existance—that there is something beyond this world. The departed descends to the lower regions by several stages. At their provision houses they have a ladder with four steps cut out of a log. A similar stairway with four steps mark the four daily stages in the journey to the other world. On the first day the departed gets as far as the first step, where he must wait one day, the second day he reaches the second stage, & so on for four days. At the bottom of this ladder are three rivers. Arrived at the first river, the departed spends one day in cleansing himself in this river, the second day he reaches the second river, the third day he reaches the third river, where he must remain a long time, cleansing and purifying himself in its waters. Finally, his friends who have preceded him, come to him & examine him to see whether he is entirely pure. He has by this time become almost or entirely transparent. If they find that he is entirely pure from all earth-stains, they take him along to the realms of the happy; if not, he is allowed to remain or drift down the stream, & no more notice is taken of him (Oswalt 1963a:73–74).

Weinland may have projected his own beliefs into this account; he was working through the trader and the trader's Russian-speaking interpreter. If indeed this is an adequate description of the Eskimo belief system, then the Eskimo's psyche does not seem so far removed from the Christian spirit. The complexity of Eskimo culture must have baffled the Moravians and allowed them at first to take a benign view of the *kashgee*.

Nevertheless, their initial tolerance gave way to severe rejection when they recognized that the Eskimo system of good and evil and the shamans who personified it were standing in the way of the Moravian conversion process. Weinland, his wife, and their Alaskan born baby had a great deal of sickness, and after two years on the Kuskokwim they returned to the States. For a year John and Edith Kilbuck were the only Moravians in Bethel. Kilbuck was a Delaware Indian and, though a third generation Christian, may have had more awareness of cultural realities than the other missionaries. Though many missionaries worked at it, he was the first to master the Yuk dialect. As Mrs. Schwalbe puts it:

> Then he began to encounter the shamans who opposed the work of the missionaries. Even as he gained a deeper knowledge of the language there came with it a fuller revelation of the powers of darkness and the superstition which held the people in its grip (Schwalbe 1951:17).

Kilbuck recognized realistically that the *kashgee* programs were indeed religious ceremonies, and hence he felt the *kashgee* and all its functions should be destroyed. Functionally he saw the *kashgee* as a religious center outside the Moravian power and that the *kashgee* would have to be replaced by the Christian church as the center of all community life in order to bring the Moravian Christian faith to the Eskimos. In a letter to Weinland in 1890 he wrote:

> You remember the *masquerades*. At the time we could not condemn them, because we were unacquainted with their nature. Now, however, that we know that they are no more than heathen rites, the one grand religious ceremony of the year, we have condemned them, and seek to suppress them (Oswalt 1963a: 76).

From then on the Moravians took a firm stand against all Eskimo ceremony, recreational or religious, and every Eskimo rite became an orgy in their eyes. The Native dance-dramas, upon which so much of the Eskimo social life and prestige depended, were anathema to the missionaries and forbidden to their converts. Mrs. Schwalbe recounts from a missionary's diary one such "dance for the dead" held in 1898.

> The necessity for some form of amusement is present with people everywhere, and the Eskimo with his inherent dramatic instincts, his desire to *move across the stage* before his fellows, pursued his creative ability in an interesting style of self-expression. But in this he all too often followed the lust of the flesh and allowed himself to be drawn deeper and deeper into the intemperate practices of superstition. . . .
> The dancers are usually girls and women in costume, wearing elaborate head dresses and carrying dancing fans. The dancing is actually genuflections of the knees and a co-ordinated movement of the body muscles as they endeavor to interpret the song in pantomime. It is often very skillfully done. Several persons occupy the floor at once but dancing alone. The body may sway, but the dancer does not move about on the floor. The muscles of the arms ripple and then jerk as they manipulate their fans. When the body sways and bends, then suddenly comes upright again, these body muscles seem to flow along with those of the arms. . . . During and after the dances, the gifts were brought into the kashige, and one or more of the chiefs made the distribution, being careful to observe certain social codes. Such was the kind of orgy that took place in the isolated village of Ougavik that winter.
> The Helmichs were perplexed and naturally discouraged. Mrs. Helmich's diary states that during the time the skies were dark and lowering, and their hearts were dark and heavy too . . . (Schwalbe 1951:77–79).

After the condemning of the *kashgee* ceremonies, the ·missionaries attacked ceremonialism at every level. The goal of change was to substitute the Moravian church as the community center, to strip the shaman of his leadership position, and to replace him with the missionary preacher and later the Native lay Christian leader in each village.

Circumstances and cultural functions may have made this change from *kashgee* to church reasonable. A potent force for change was of course the unswerving conviction of the Moravians that fulfillment and salvation could come only through Christian conversion. Later we may observe secular White teachers among the Eskimo teaching with the same consistent zeal that the "good life" can come only through conversion to White values, which basically are supported by Christian conventions. The *kashgee* as a community center, the Eskimos' own mystical belief in good and bad spirits, their belief in afterlife, all appeared, at least superficially, not to be in conflict with Christianity.

One major difference between the two systems was the position of women. The *kashgee* ceremonialism and Eskimo mystique in general reinforced a subordinate position of women. The Moravians on the other hand offered women an equal or at least coordinate role in religious ceremony and sanctions. The Moravian women, whether married or single women, were missionaries in their own right. A reflection of this can be seen today in the village churches; women and children often make up the backbone of the congregation and men may come infrequently or only on special occasions of celebration. So Moravian Christianity, reversing the situation of the pagan *kashgee,* supported the women's role and criticized the men's role. This applied significantly to the separation of the sexes. The *kashgee* was essentially the separate dwelling place of men. Here they gathered for relaxation and sought strength and status in the heat baths. The *kashgee* was the men's house, and women entered only to bring the men food and on invitation to take part in general ceremonies; the rest of the time the women stayed in their own dwellings waiting for the men to come to them. The Moravians considered this morally wrong. In the eyes of the Moravians the family should live together as a unit and the Eskimo dwelling was not a home until it contained the Christian family unit of husband, wife, and children. Of course anything less than lifetime marital fidelity was proscribed as sin.

Over the years the church came to replace the *kashgee,* both as a building and as a community gathering place; the house became a home, a family dwelling place; and the heat baths of the *kashgee* were replaced by the smaller private steam bath houses, adopted from the *banjas* of the Russian traders. Here parts of the *kashgee* functions were carried on. Men continued to be avid bathers, and the *banjas* are still a major focus of sociability; with the changing status of women achieved through Christian communization, the *banjas* today are used by both men and women.

Within the *kashgee* the block to change was the shaman. Despite the division between male and female roles, some of the shamans were women. Kilbuck saw the shamans as frauds, as well as agents of the devil, because they used tricks to create magic. Shamans frequently claimed they made trips to the moon, when actually all they did was sit on top of the *kashgee*. Kilbuck's attack on them was to unmask them as frauds, again striking at the very heart of Eskimo mystique and wisdom.

Priests of many religions—Navajo singers, Zuni priests, medicine men of many tribes—indulge in ceremonial acts technically involving tricks; so, it might be said, does the Catholic priest conducting the Mass. What missionaries label as trickery often may be acts of symbolism by which the religious needs of the group may be fulfilled. It is a question whether the magical tricks of the Eskimo shamans were not understood by the Eskimos themselves as religious charades and accepted nonetheless as symbolic. The tricks as observed by the missionaries were also ritual, and ritual formalizes the style of the culture. Medicine men, shamans, religious leaders in general, are usually intellectual leaders among their people with keen mystical and psychological insights invaluable to the group and with practical functions as well, such as keeping track of the seasons and predicting the weather. Hence attacking the shamans as frauds also insulted the intellectual integrity of village leaders, possibly leading to significant deterioration in the effectiveness of Native leadership.

The Moravians, though strangers to the life and death balance of the Arctic environment, figuratively took over the role of the shaman. The question that must be answered in terms of the modern well-being of the Eskimos is: Have the Christian ministers realistically been able to lead the Eskimos into a fruitful harmonious existence with their ecology as did the Native spiritual leaders? As significantly we must also question whether the White schoolhouse has adequately replaced the *kashgee* as a school for a fulfilled survival in the Arctic village and ecology. Moravian White education offered the Eskimos survival by technologically mastering nature and environment whereas the Native shaman offered survival by achieving an equilibrium with the forces of nature. Hence White schools are oppositional to Eskimo mystical as well as technological relationship to his environment. The school has replaced the *kashgee,* but does not offer Eskimos a life center that this communal gathering place offered the traditional village.

Certainly the missionaries were dedicated teachers, willing to risk their lives to bring their conception of enlightenment to the Eskimos. John Kilbuck, by kayak and dog sled, visited the most remote villages. His generosity, friendliness, and also practical medical skills made him welcome wherever he went. Yet the missionaries' progress was discouragingly slow, in part because the Moravians did not consider conversion an easy process. Where the Russian Orthodox had been content with immediate baptism, the Moravians required of the communicants a high degree of conscientious instruction in Christian precepts and commitment. In the third year eight Eskimos were admitted into full membership in the church. All of these had been baptized earlier in the Orthodox church, yet Kilbuck held them off for a year after they had first asked for membership, testing their consciences and preparing them for this important step. Kilbuck wanted complete conversion and complete rejection of pagan Eskimo self and also "a profession of faith in the Triune God," for interpretation of the doctrine of the trinity was a major point of theological difference between Orthodox and European Protestant beliefs (Oswalt 1963a:75).

The Moravians appeared as disturbed by some aspects of Russian Orthodoxy and Catholicism as they were of outright paganism. In the eyes of the mission they may have looked the same, and understandably so. Eskimo paganism was deeply rooted in animism, mystery, and the forces of nature. Russian Orthodoxy built its strength on pageantry and mystery and was able to align itself harmoniously with the nature worship of the Eskimos. This has its counterpart in the Catholic missions in the American Southwest that have also related peacefully across the mysteries of Pueblo Indian nature-oriented worship. The Moravian's insistence on total surrender of Eskimo self slowed the conversion of the Eskimos, for the Eskimo personality was inexplicably bound up with their total relationship to their natural surroundings.

The Kilbucks must have felt the cultural wall between the missionaries and the Native self. The Eskimos came to the mission friendly and grateful, accepted Christian kindness, and then retreated into the pagan darkness of the villages. How could the Gospel carry across this gulf? One method was the initiation of the "helper" program, enlisting the dedication of converted Eskimos to carry Christianity into their own villages. The first two helpers were consecrated by the Moravian bishop on his visit to the mission field in 1891. Several villages had been singled out for intensive proselytizing, and to each of these a helper was appointed. These men aided in the church services and influenced fellow villagers to accept the Christian teachings. They became the eyes and the ears of the missionaries, reporting every strength and weakness, who was ready for conversion, and who was slipping away. The missionaries would then make personal visits to these members. The helpers worked right alongside Kilbuck in his preaching, supporting the lesson of the sermon wherever his command of the Eskimo language broke down. This innovation greatly accelerated Christian education and opened the door to sweeping changes within the villages. For example, the village of Kwethluk, under the pressure of a vigorous religious helper, was persuaded to burn all their ceremonial masks. The Moravians would indeed have been slow in reaching the Eskimo heart without the aid of the religious helpers. Several Eskimos were ordained as ministers in the early years. Today Native assistants who are called lay pastors are still the core of church strength in the villages.

A high point of success came when the son of a famous shaman, trained to follow in his father's power, joined the helper program. Helper Neck appeared to be an exceptional example of a Native who did move from a leader role in Eskimo culture to leadership and responsibility within the Christian value system without losing the integrity and effectiveness of his Eskimo personality. He retained his special position of insight and influence and dedicated himself to overthrowing the shamans' power, fighting fire with fire. The missionaries referred to him as "the Apostle to the Eskimo." Helper Neck devised his own intricate system of writing to present Christian teachings in the Eskimo language and taught the system to his co-workers. He was the earliest and probably the most outstanding Native teacher among the Kuskokwim Eskimos.

The Moravians seized upon the value of Native teachers to spread the Gospel, but they did not reason from there that Natives could also be instructors in their White schools as well. We have no record of Natives being used in the classroom in the effective way that the Eskimo helpers were used to carry out grassroots Christian education in the villages. We appreciate that from the beginning schooling centered around teaching English as a means of reading and writing, and Eskimos would have had to master English before they could function as English teachers. But if the Moravians had appreciated that Eskimo teachers teaching in Eskimo could have been as persuasive and effective as Helper Neck in presenting concepts, they might have summoned the patience to train educational collaborators as well.

SHIFTING ECONOMIC CURRENTS

We cannot consider the human effect of the American take-over of Alaska without a careful look at where the Eskimos appeared to be in 1884 when the first Moravian missionaries arrived on the Kuskokwim. Earlier reports make it appear the Eskimos changed very little under Russian influence. Weinland and

Hartman, like Sheldon Jackson before them, were shocked at the "plight" of the Eskimos, probably a shared response of culture shock at the severe life style of the Eskimos. Some eighty years later Edward Kennedy stood on the banks of the Kuskokwim and expressed the same shock at the simplicity of the Eskimo village. In sincerity he too saw Eskimo life style as poverty.

There is little evidence that the spiritual and social structure of the river Eskimos had changed or decayed appreciably. The *kashgee* described by Zagoskin and the *kashgee* described by Weinland forty years later were the same, except that the giving away ceremonies had been enriched by new trade items. Within the twenty-year period between the departure of the Russians and the arrival of the Moravians, the general economy of the Kuskokwim had begun a process of economic and commercial change that has continued accelerating into the still unresolved conflict of contemporary Eskimo life in Alaska.

To discuss the changes that began with the American purchase of Alaska we must trace through economic variables and speculate on the effectiveness of missionary education to equip the Eskimos to meet the invasion of American commercial values into their lives then and now. Certainly the Russian American Fur Company began this invasion, but within a different cycle of history and by a different cultural style that rested with little conflict on the structure of the Eskimo village. When the San Francisco-based Alaskan Commerical Company took over the operations, traders and trading culture changed too. The influence was not from imperial Czarist Russia via Siberia but from the aggressive development of the United States.

In 1884 when the first Moravian missionaries, Weinland and Hartmann, arrived to explore the area for a mission site, there were three thriving posts on the Kuskokwim, all owned by the Alaskan Commerical Company. Trade was lucrative, and Weinland was shocked by the evident exploitation of the Eskimos by oppressively high markup on trade goods and the bare subsistence pay for Eskimo labor offered at the posts and for paddling or lining large skin boats loaded with trade goods up the river from seagoing vessels anchored in the Kuskokwim Bay.

At that time the Alaska Commerical Company operations on the Kuskokwim were run by a Russian Finn named Separe, with a total monopoly of all trading on the river. In the pattern of trade with Native peoples everywhere, the traders made a two-fold profit, first from the sale of furs on the world market, and again from mark-up on the merchandize they traded to the Eskimos and Indians. For a brief period Separe became an independent trader with a newly formed company. While this competition was going on, the price paid for furs soared, and as an additional inducement to hold trade the Eskimos were extended open credit. Then when the competing company withdrew and Separe returned to the Alaska Commercial Company, the price dropped immediately and credit was rigorously discouraged again.

With the discovery of gold in the upper Yukon in the 1890s all of Alaska felt the impact of the fever. Though no significant fields were found in the Kuskokwim, the movement of prospectors and speculators of all kinds brought a rapid change as the commercial White world moved into the Eskimo domain. Trapping eventually become so profitable that White trappers began to invade the Eskimo trapping grounds. As a measure of change, the price of a mink pelt, which was 25¢

in 1900, had risen to $4 by 1906. In 1907 a combine of eight White trappers garnered $30,000 worth of mink. The trading economy must have continued affecting Eskimo life patterns by encouraging heads of families to stay on the trap lines rather than return nightly to the sociability of the *kashgee* or to their family circles. Traded fur filled life with countless new items, and commercialization began shifting the cultural base of Eskimo life. By 1910 there were radical changes in the pattern of Eskimo communities and probably significant changes in the values of the people.

Another measure of economic change was a late potlatch in Bethel, one of the largest gift-giving ceremonies on record, and one of the last. A semiannual missionary report on the activities at Bethel contained this observation:

> Good as the above may seem (referring to the high fur prices and the quantities of trade goods in Bethel), there is nevertheless the unpleasant feature about the sudden prosperity of our people. We hope that this will be as short-lived as were the temporary high prices of fur. One of the unpleasant features for the missionaries was the great "give-away" dance among three villages, which was held in Bethel. At this particular dance (there were others elsewhere) goods of all sorts were bought or collected and brought into the kashigi where they awaited their disposal. There were several nights of dancing, entertaining and visiting. Then, on the last day and night, this accumulated material was given away, the greater portion falling to the entertaining village. Most of the people received some flour, some got seal oil, or skins for boots, rifles, stoves or cloth. It was estimated that at this particular dance about twenty thousand dollars worth of goods were given or danced away. Perhaps there was little actual waste, still we remonstrate because of unfairness and unwholesome tendencies which this practice leads to (Oswalt 1963a:82).

On one hand the Eskimos were making huge profits for the Alaskan Commerical Company trading posts. On the other, Eskimos were for the first time dealing in conspicuous consumption. The first response was to siphon off the wealth in prestige potlatches to raise the status of the village. The second response unquestionably was an accelerated acculturation and change, which Eskimos as well as Indians have had a hard time ordering constructively. The response of the Moravians was to pray for falling fur prices so that the process of Christian moral conversion could continue uninterrupted.

Moravian records speak unhappily of the invasion of miners and accompanying commercial entrepreneurs around the turn of the century. The mission tried to be hospitable, but was unquestionably glad when this rush of prosperous strangers ended. On the other hand, the Alaska Commercial Company was a respected partner in bringing Christianity to the Eskimos. Mr. Lind, the trader at Bethel who was a Finn and a Lutheran with an Eskimo wife, saw great value in the missionaries and was continually helpful and supportive.

Of course the missionaries saw their function as very different from the traders', but in perspective they were similar and complementary agents of change. Despite disapproval of commercial exploitation, the Moravians themselves became traders, partly at the invitation of the Eskimos. In Eskimo eyes all White men wanted to prosper by dealing in Eskimo furs. The Moravians described most of their operations in detail, except for their trading, which they mention with an apology for mixing commerce with Christian conscience. One statement to the mission board in

Bethlehem points out that trading was a survival necessity to get food—which it was—and to pay the overhead of the Arctic mission—which may have been sheer opportunism.

Practically they had to work hand in glove with the Alaska Commercial Company, for their survival depended on the company's goodwill. Pragmatically and culturally they had to work in harmony. So from the beginning the Moravians have always cooperated with business enterprise on the Kuskokwim. This made them symbolically and economically a unit of the White enterprise in the Arctic. By 1900 the pattern of exploitation of the Natives was well established. White men were looking for gold along the Kuskokwim tributaries and trapping the hunting ground of the river Eskimos. What did or could the Moravians do about this invasion? In terms of directed education for the self-determination of the Eskimos, the mold of education was cast, and Moravian education continued to direct itself to the moral basis of Eskimo society without effectively involving themselves with Eskimo economic survival. There was, however, one action period of realistic vocational Arctic education, created by the introduction of reindeer from Lapland.

It was Sheldon Jackson who seized upon reindeer herding as a solution for Eskimo development. He had made the first report to the U.S. Office of Education on the state of Native welfare, and his concern had won him the appointment as special commissioner of education for the Territory of Alaska. As mentioned he was appalled by the Eskimo life and determined to help. He was also a realistic economic observer and noted the increasing presence of White trappers and the general effect of material change created by the sale of furs. He must have seen that the economic future for the Eskimos was precarious unless they got a more stable economic base than trapping. He saw reindeer herding as a source of food, clothing, and profit for the Eskimos.

Jackson's reindeer project got under way in 1892 among the Eskimos of the north coast. As a service directly under the U.S. Office of Education, the administration of the program was placed in the hands of the schools, many of which were missionary enterprises in those early days. In 1901 the Bethel Moravian mission acquired a herd of 176, followed by another group of 200. By 1904 the deer in the Bethel area numbered over a thousand, and the Moravians were realistically, for the first time, involved in the economic development of business education for the Eskimos.

It took special training to herd and manage the reindeer. Lapp herders came along with herds and stayed, first as instructors to the Alaskans but later as reindeer owners. An apprenticeship system was established in which selected Eskimo youths were assigned to the herders. In turn they would be given reindeer and become individual herders themselves. These apprentices had to have special training in reading, writing, and bookkeeping to succeed in their role, and this created an action curriculum in the Moravian School at Bethel to train Eskimos to succeed in realistic Arctic skills and economy.

Anna Schwalbe speaks nostalgically of the school of the reindeer apprentices:.

Often these swarthy young men may have felt out of place spending hours at undersized desks, trying to re-acquaint themselves with textbooks and pencils rather than handling lassos and other gear in the great wintry out-of-doors. Nevertheless, they were the envy of the little school boys and the lions of the other sex. On the day of their arrival in the village at the first sound of the little tinkling bells or the appearance of antlers on the horizon line, the cry of "Dundit, dundit" (the deer! the deer!) caused boys and girls to stampede pell mell from the schoolroom. Sometimes shy little sons and daughters, children of the herders, were in the train, coming to attend school, remaining in the home of some relative or with the missionary until the close of the term. These little folk were generally better dressed than the village children, wearing beautiful parkas with wide trimming bands in intricate design made by a loving mother's hands (Schwalbe 1951:137).

Here is an account of spontaneous Native-oriented education that appeared relevant to Eskimo survival and self appreciation. Here White teachers were integrated into an Eskimo economy. Moravian teachers near the reindeer herding not only instructed the herders in keeping books but were also responsible for making inspections of the herds and turning in annual counts of the deer. Moravian education at this time was genuinely involved in one practical aspect of Eskimo environmental survival. Anna Schwalbe considered this a vital period in Moravian service and successful education, saying, "All of this, then, concerning the reindeer has resulted in an education which may be said to have served the Eskimo well, the effects being more far reaching than we can now see" (1951:137).

This innovation in education came after several decades of American commercial interaction on the Kuskokwim. There had already been a serious invasion of Eskimo life that had succeeded in giving the Eskimo a compliant role to the ever increasing White culture. Reindeer herding might have become a model for motivating the villages ideally into economic leadership, but for various reasons what developed was the concentration of the herds in the hands of White businessmen and Lapps, including the mission and the government, with the Eskimos in a subordinate capacity as hired herders. Though reindeer herding represented a substantial industry for thirty years, a combination of factors—the airplane, wartime employment, vagaries of the market, wolves, as well as sociocultural factors of Eskimo village life—led to the decline and virtual disappearance of the deer from the Kuskokwim.[5] White education returned to its original role of focusing on Christian morality, hygiene, and survival in the lifeways of White people. Trapping continued into the 1960s as a major source of financial revenue, but as Sheldon Jackson may have predicted, it has failed to give a secure base for Eskimo economic survival.

MISSIONARY FOUNDATION
OF WHITE EDUCATION FOR ESKIMOS

The Moravian mission's moral position clearly laid down the shape of White education for the Kuskokwim Eskimos. Hence when we consider the process and effect of Moravian education in Christianity and basic White skills, we are looking at the current of what may still be happening today. Moravian education followed consistently the pattern of education for Native Americans as far back as its history can be traced.

[5] See also Lantis 1952:127–148.

*Moravian Christianity is the center of community life in most Kuskokwim villages
and the basis for education.*

Throughout the New World missionaries were the first White educators to the
Native Americans. In 1636 in Quebec the Jesuits opened what was probably the
first school for Indians of the Northeast, a boarding school for the Huron tribe.
As usual, recruiting of neophytes was the first obstacle. Parkman recounts this
first effort:

> . . . Father Daniel, descending from the Huron country, worn, emaciated, his
> cassock patched and tattered, and his shirt in rags, brought with him a boy, to
> whom two others were soon added; and through the influence of the interpreter,
> Nicollet, the number was afterwards increased by several more. One of them
> ran away, two ate themselves to death, a fourth was carried home by his father,
> while three of those remaining stole a canoe, loaded it with all they could lay
> their hands upon, and escaped in triumph with their plunder (Parkman 1898:
> 260).

Moravian educators fared far better than this, but the problems they had to
overcome remain basically unsolved today. The Moravians, too, had a hard time
recruiting their early students. Edith Kilbuck wrote of the problems of founding
this first school:

In our second year we opened a school. We had a great deal of trouble in getting scholars. Parents said they would not send their children to school; they would die if they dwelt with white people, and if they had their hair cut, their noses would bleed; or we would feed them with salt, and then medicine men would have no power over them, should they get sick. . . . They asked us why we wanted them to go to school. How much would we give them? What price would we pay for a boy's time? (Oswalt 1963*a*:35).

Even at this early date White schooling was running up against structure invisible to the educators. Because boys away from home were not doing their chores, someone else had to do their work for them, so the parents should be paid for loaning their children to the school!

Yet from the outset of White education, it has been the student who has had to change to become educated. From the beginning of the Moravians' first school in 1886 the lessons were taught in English. This may have impeded education in the broadest sense, but teaching English symbolized bringing the Eskimos a new style of life. It was inconceivable to the missionaries that the Moravian school should adopt elements from Eskimo life; this would have been contrary to getting educated. From the beginning Eskimo children had to give up their own ways to accept what the White teacher had to offer. They had to accept a rigid schedule in conflict with their sense of time and program. Children ran away, and those who stayed had to change their style of life radically. Even in this early beginning Native education *had to be* a subtractive process; to *add* to the net sum of the Eskimo child would have allowed the pagan spirit to live on within. The Native child had to be purged of his original sin to accept the amenities of Christian civilization.

Moral as well as temporal values were forced upon the Eskimo students—White morality that at this time related in no way to Eskimo life. Students were whipped for disobedience, which must have been a great shock since Eskimos disciplined their children by nonviolent means. Subsistence activities of families were seriously interfered with, for parents were loath to make trips to traplines and fishing camps without their children. These journeys were essential to survival, yet teachers felt that children should stay behind for school. The Moravians, many of whom came from rural backgrounds and were sensitive to the realities of subsistence cycles, were willing to make adjustments that would meet some of the demands of seasonal subsistence migrations. But federal and territorial school administrations were less flexible, and then and now the pressure is to make the school year conform to that of the lower states (Anderson and Eells 1935:296–297). Thus, from the beginning, White education has plucked the child out of his ecological life and education and directed him away from his Native environment.

By the turn of the century the U.S. Office of Education, an agency of the Department of the Interior, was partially overseeing the Kuskokwim schools. The government paid for equipment used and paid salaries, but the teachers' salaries were given to the mission, which in turn gave the missionary teachers a Moravian stipend. For the federally supported schools here and elsewhere in Alaska general policies and curricula were laid down by a superintendent stationed in Seattle. The contracts called for instructions, first of all in sanitation and then the three R's, so mission teachers felt justified in prohibiting Native customs that they found objectionable. A teacher in 1907 strongly objected to the smell of fur clothing in the classroom, so even at that early date White clothing had to be obtained for the Eskimo children (Schwalbe 1951:104). The curriculum called for sewing classes for the girls. The teacher wisely appreciated that the Eskimos were far more adept at sewing then she was, so the period was turned over to the older girls and the students were taught to make towels and handkerchiefs, many of which were sent away to mission groups in the states, presumably to be sold for aid to the mission. Apparently Eskimo-style stitchery and beadwork were not sent along with the "hankies" (Schwalbe 1951:106). There is no explanation for this choice of handiwork for the mission societies back home.

It is important that the first requisite of federally directed education was hygiene. From the first Moravian contact the Eskimos' unconcern for sanitation was a major point of shock. The missionaries were fearful of contracting diseases from the Natives, and exposed themselves to the unwashed bodies and lice only as a necessary sacrifice required by their zeal to uplift the Eskimos in both body and soul. Yet, before the White man came to the Kuskokwim there were few contagious diseases (Anderson and Eells 1935:65). What the missionaries saw as lack of hygienic custom in reality reflected the absence of certain types of physical illness. Western hygiene has been developed to guard against particular illnesses; if we had no tradition of sickness relating to germs, we might have no values in hygiene.

The Eskimos had an entirely different conception of disease. They recognized illness that exterminated whole villages as catastrophe brought on by the White men. Smallpox swept western Alaska in 1838–39, and the Eskimos burned the settlement called Russian Mission on the Yukon in revenge. A Moravian census made in 1890 revealed that 50 percent of all Eskimos had some chronic diseases, and a large portion of the children did not reach adulthood. Death always stalked the Arctic villages in accidents and hunger, but apparently by 1890 White diseases —smallpox, tuberculosis, whooping cough, influenza—were well established in the Arctic. Ironically, one of the appeals of the missionaries was their ability to treat White diseases that the shamans were unable to cure. In 1896 there was an epidemic of whooping cough on the Kuskokwim, and mortality among the Native children was very high. In the same period influenza swept away half the population of the region. Hygiene was then a mortal necessity, and a major function and power of the missionaries was treating diseases that the mission itself may have been instrumental in bringing into the Arctic. Diseases and economic disruption came to Alaska with White progress, and so, pragmatically, White education should be able to meet these disasters by special training and sophistication gained through White learning.

The advance of Christianity might be seen as illness and disorganization of Native equilibrium, but of course missionaries were just one of the agencies of change in the Arctic. Sheldon Jackson bitterly recognized that White enterprise had seriously upset the Eskimos, and he saw the missions as the only positive White force that might balance the damage already done. We must see the Moravians' mission of change in the total context of the White invasion of the Arctic. The Moravians had a long tradition of missionary work, including work with Eskimos in Greenland, and may well have been the best prepared teachers of

Native people in the 1880s. But of course they were White teachers with White solutions, and our interest in their program is basically this content.

After the Moravians' pioneer school was opened in Bethel in 1886, their program was extended to other villages up and down the river, on the coast of Kuskokwim Bay, and on the Nushagak River to the east. As the Alaska Territory developed, the federal government gradually built up a network of schools for Natives, for many years working in close collaboration with the missionaries, appointing missionary or "missionary-minded" teachers to the village schools. Increased bureaucratic intervention certainly must have made Eskimo schooling even more rigid, along with the missionary goals that were firmly implanted in the curriculum. Native education throughout Alaska was administered the same way, parceling out school support to the various mission programs. The missionary heritage also pervades the education of American Indians and still affects Bureau of Indian Affairs schools throughout the country today. For example, at the new $12-million boarding school at Dilcon on the Navajo Reservation in 1968, the principal and 60 percent of the teaching staff were Mennonites.

Indigenous people all have schooling for survival, for subsistence, for defense, and for psychic resilience to deal with often harsh environment. This intense education does not necessarily take place in the home, for often communal patterns do not give the nuclear family this responsibility. Eskimos on the Kuskokwim and elsewhere along the western sea coast of Alaska did not have home and family culture as westerners conceive of them. The *barabarrah* was for women (often two or more) and their children. For the men and the growing boys living, in various dimensions, circulated around a communal dwelling. As described, men worked, ate, relaxed, and slept in the *kashgee*. It was the beginning and the end of their days. Boys grew to manhood in the *kashgee*. And so, before the *kashgee* became a church, it was a school.

We observe that Eskimo parents are very permissive with their children, especially their sons. Domestic process in the home educated the girls and taught them to rear children, to cook and to assist in the processing of fish, meat, and furs. But traditionally the men had little work to do in the home; all intellectual pursuits and most manufacturing activities took place in the *kashgee*. Hence the home was not a place for discipline or learning male skills. Home was a place to play, to love your children. The Eskimo father could do this loving without restraint, for the boys would be dealt with in the *kashgee* and disciplined *by all the men of the community*.

Formal school was not in the home, and schooling was for boys, not for girls. In many societies this has been the case; even in European Renaissance culture schooling was only for boys (Ong 1963:444–466). Among the Eskimos the *kashgee* was for men and boys only, and girls had to receive their education spontaneously in the life process.

The *kashgee* could be compared to the longhouse on the Olympic Peninsula which was also the school of the community where boys were disciplined. The longhouse itself has perished from parents' memory, but parents continue to be very permissive. A school principal suggested that a mother should exercise more control over her daughter, who had been suspended for truancy. The mother agreed but later expressed her wonder, "Why do they want me to make her go to school if they can't get her to stay there?" (Barnhardt 1970:54–57).

The White school is not a longhouse or a *kashgee*. It is remote from the village influence of the men and not involved with the day to day survival of the village. The White school in this dimension can be seen as an extreme contradiction of Eskimo Native learning.

The Eskimo style of indirect instruction or correction of error, technical or social, appears as one of positive reinforcement. When a boy kills his first game, there is rejoicing and a special feast; nothing is said about the game that got away. When a girl cleans her first salmon or picks her first bucket of berries there is equal rejoicing and feasting. Both in social control and practical instruction there is present a constant concern *not to embarrass or unnecessarily discourage the learner*. This restraint carries over to allow the learner or the individual to ignore a request when he does not wish to comply. Children do not, in this way, refuse to honor their parents' order; rather, they do not acknowledge that they hear the command. *This does not embarrass the parent or attack his position.* This behavior is characteristic of other societies. Spindler (1963:351–399) described a similar attitude in Menomini education, where criticisms are implied rather than forcefully stated.

This is also the style of social control among Eskimo adults. In the village of Napaskiak on the Kuskokwim the village council regulates antisocial behavior by implicitly influencing the miscreant to change his own ways. If this fails they suggest forcefully that he leave the village (Oswalt 1963b:69–70). But circumstances are rare when an individual would be humiliated in order to correct his behavior. Apparently it would take an extreme situation for the villagers to purge the wrongdoer publicly. There are indeed records of instances of hysteria where destructive individuals were stoned to death by the group, but this is pathological behavior.

During World War II the Alaska Territorial Guard was organized for possible defense of Alaska. Village leaders were made officers and younger men enlisted; uniforms and equipment were issued freely, and the discipline usually associated with White military establishments was not of prime concern. Consequently what developed was a practical, paternalistic arrangement in which the villagers wore their uniforms daily and used the rifles for hunting. After the war the organization was replaced by the National Guard of the U.S. Army. Oswalt describes the situation in Napaskiak. Direction of the Guard was taken away from the village elders and given to young Eskimo sergeants, those who could communicate in English with their Army superiors. Learning was reversed, and to the shock of the whole village, grown men were shouted at for minor drill infractions, and worse, young men were shouting commands at old people. Oswalt feels this was a traumatic experience for all the village. Here was a blunt change from Eskimo education to White-style instruction and control! (Oswalt 1963b:69–70).

When the Eskimo dwelling became a family home shared by the man of the family and the *kashgee* function came to be replaced by the white schoolhouse, education for survival took place only in the field. The home, for children, remained a permissive and tranquil environment. The White school took over the harsher disciplining of the child in both moral and academic excellence. The style of learning and discipline was in opposition to the home and the village world of the children, which, quite aside from curriculum, may have added to the distance between the White school and the Eskimo community.

Outside the school Eskimo boys continued to learn Eskimo skills in the survival process by direct participation in a task—mending a sled, stretching pelts for drying, netting salmon, setting traps and snares. But very early in White schooling, school attendance cut across the subsistence processes of hunting, trapping, fishing, and berry picking. White scheduling and curriculum had problems in accommodating this environmental education. And the more bureaucratically organized the schools became, the deeper they intruded on the learning opportunity of tundra and river. Often when the families needed their children most, they were sitting in school rather than learning to participate in the work culture of their villages. Later, at the threshold of manhood, village students who want to go beyond the eighth grade must leave for faraway boarding high schools, some going as far as Oklahoma. Yet, in a report of Eskimo education in the late fifties, Alaskan educators were proposing to keep the Eskimo children in educational camps through the summer, the most important period of salmon fishing (Ray 1959).

In 1917 a Territorial Department of Education was established which developed schools "for white children and those of mixed blood leading a civilized life" (Anderson and Eells 1935:215). Bethel was granted such a school in 1923 (Schwalbe 1951:166). Though never absolute, this was essentially segregation on both a racial and a cultural basis. The territorial schools were the forerunners of the present state schools. The federal schools, chiefly seen as schools for Natives, were shifted from the Office of Education to the Office (later Bureau) of Indian Affairs in 1931.

The impact of White schools on Eskimo learning affected not only style and content but also the method and focus of learning. Traditional Eskimo learning was fundamentally a training in observation and the analysis of this sensory reception. Content was frequently nonverbal and ecological in experience—weather prediction, ice prediction, warnings of blizzards, the drift of game. White learning shifted attention to the verbal and the literate, which had survival value in abstract circumstances usually unrelated to the natural world surrounding the school. Humanly, the instructors' role was shifted from village men to strangers teaching content administered from Seattle and Washington, D.C.

When the Moravians opened their first school in 1886, they taught the Eskimo children in the only fashion understood and acceptable in those days. When the federal government took more direct responsibility for Native education in the succeeding decades, the concept of educating Native people did not change appreciably. By 1931 when Native education was shifted from the U.S. Office of Education to the Bureau of Indian Affairs major changes in philosophy were rocking the larger field of American education. But, as within the BIA, these developments were from the top down and rarely reached the grassroots school or changed the formal shape of public education. Paralleling this consciousness was a growing awareness that American Indian education was already in difficulties. In answer, radical new methods were proposed and tried. Was this going to change

Home of the Postmaster in Tuluksak (middle income).

White education for the Eskimo people? There are of course many factors and drives establishing the character of schools, so that radical change, even within the controlled program of the BIA, has proved to be difficult.

During the thirties the BIA introduced a new approach of Native cultural determination that shifted the emphasis away from boarding schools toward community-oriented day schools in an effort to bring grassroots education to Native people. This effort coincided with a sweeping civil rights law, the Indian Reorganization Act, which was written to give Native Americans administrative control over their own destiny. This act directed even more energy into day schools as centers of community development, and BIA teachers were recruited to help Native communities organize into self-governing organizations with activities centering around the school. This program enlisted a new character of teachers who directively and nondirectively reversed, if only temporarily, some of the historical goals of missionary education.

Such developments could have resolved many educational problems and opened the door to community development. Many dedicated teachers with zeal equal to the spirit of the early Moravian teachers struggled to redirect the course of BIA education. Certainly they were in conflict with missionary goals, but maybe even more seriously they were in conflict with many of their own White values and the pressures of accelerating progress in Alaska. The program opened a contest between the traditional goals of Christian zeal and Native self-development, between collective White American conformity and Eskimo difference.

The educational program of the Indian New Deal may have come too late to salvage the destruction of a century of miseducation. Many of the ethnically ideal

goals of this plan attempted to involve Native survival culture that had become increasingly dysfunctional. At the other extreme, the community school program may have come thirty years too soon. Such schemes today would be welcomed by many Indian groups who are now much more sophisticated about their identity and concerned with cultural determinism.

Missionary and White education, historically and still today, remains blurred in relation to goals for Eskimo survival. The community school renaissance of the BIA program of the thirties tried to clear this educational vision. But the over-reach of modern cultural supremacy places Eskimo education today in a position not very different from that of the Moravian school of 1900.

ESKIMO SOCIETY TODAY AND THE PATTERN OF CHANGE

The tundras of the Kuskokwim remained in great isolation through nearly a century and a half of White European influence. Change began imperceptibly with the arrival of the Russian traders, but the pace of change accelerated steadily with each new wave of White intruders. Change speeded considerably under the Christian education of the Moravians, but still the relative isolation of the area allowed the Eskimos to accommodate the challenging influences into their own life style. The pressure of White intrusion increased as transportation and communication breached the isolation of the tundra. More trading posts were built, the Kuskokwim River was charted, and deep water vessels could discharge their cargos directly on the river bank at Bethel. Wendell Oswalt feels that by 1925 the indigenous life style, with its belief in the pagan supernatural, was gone for good from the culture of the river Eskimos.

Along the river, village patterns had changed also by this date. Gone were the *barabarrah* sod-covered igloos, though sod dwellings persisted in isolated tundra villages into the 1930s. Gone were the *kashgee* communal centers—either burned down or torn down; the last, in Napaskiak, was burned in 1950. By 1935 village patterns changed further under the organizing influence of the BIA school and community program. BIA teachers had the educational responsibility of organizing village leadership to accommodate the opportunities offered in the Indian Reorganization Act. The villages for the first time developed governing councils. Many BIA teachers worked zealously to effect community development on many levels, so in a sense this was a period of genuine community education. During this period, on their own initiative, teachers introduced electricity generating plants to some villages, improved water supplies, and even stimulated the forming of a cooperative store, as in the village of Kwethluk. At a later date teachers in the isolated tundra community of Nunapichuk helped develop the first fishing cooperative, which later formed the foundation of the successful fishing cooperative at Bethel that today affects the welfare of many Kuskokwim communities. In 1918 when reindeer herding was at its peak the federal government built a hospital at Akiak, the herding center. Two years later it was moved to its present location in Bethel.

The Second World War suddenly ended the isolation of the Kuskokwim and ushered in the state of rapid change that is the character of Eskimo life today. The proximity of the Japanese enemy sealed off the Kuskokwim on one level, closed schools, and interfered with social interaction. War hysteria brought violent turmoil and also at least one example of human futility. The one Japanese citizen of Bethel, whose skills helped build defensive army installations there, was summarily separated from his Eskimo family and deported to a concentration camp in California, where he died (Schwalbe 1951:243).

At the same time the wartime drama filled the Eskimo world with thousands of White military men and dumped tons of goods and technology on the river banks of the tundra. Eskimos saw White skills transform boggy tundra into expansive air fields and also witnessed the White man's material affluence used, stored, or discarded as expendable waste. Much that was thrown away entered the Eskimo community, and the bulldozers, motorized transportation, and vast technology entered the Eskimos' consciousness and expectations. This turmoil is still the character of Bethel, the important air hub of western Alaska, an expanding city of White enterprise in the Arctic.

The war recruited the Eskimo villagers into scouting units and later into units of the National Guard. Oswalt feels that this postwar development was the largest single influence in changing the structure of the Eskimo village. The National Guard gave ample equipment and prestige to its men and placed the administration of all this activity in the National Guard Headquarters in Bethel. This unquestionably diminished the prestige and leadership of the newly formed village councils and made young men more prestigious than the old. The Guard brought obsolescence into the villages and linked the values of the village with the other White world. It would be distortive not to appreciate that the National Guard also contributed to village organization, further educated the adult population, and gave the men special technological training. But positively or negatively, it broke the isolation that had given each village its own destiny.

Wendell Oswalt's two studies of the Kuskokwim, taken together, offer details of both change and continuity. In *Mission of Change in Alaska* he traces the pervasive influence of the Moravian missionaries who in the forty years between 1885 and 1925 managed to bring an end to major manifestations of classical Eskimo culture. Yet in *Napaskiak: An Alaskan Eskimo Community* Oswalt reports details of a great deal of Eskimo culture that was surprisingly unchanged. Napaskiak, six miles downstream from Bethel, came through World War II still retaining much of its man-to-nature relationships as well as many ritual patterns of Eskimo culture. Probably the beliefs behind these rituals had faded but the ceremonies went on. Growing up in Napaskiak still required many traditional rites of passage. Male-female relationships, patterns of marriage, and the dignity of growing old persisted in the traditional way. There were still two shamans, an old man and a young girl who had "the power of healing." At least in Napaskiak this apparently created no conflict.

Significantly Napaskiak is a Russian Orthodox village. It was among the first communities that the Moravians tried to convert, but for unclear reasons they failed. Was this because Napaskiak was a recognized mystical center and so was able to repel the missionaries? More likely it was an especially self-contained organization and resented the particular pressures of the Moravians. Though the Russian Orthodox Church was not active in the Kuskokwim when the Moravians arrived, something of the earlier tradition persisted and was contrasted in the Native mind with different emphases of the Moravians. In 1905 a visiting Russian priest baptized half of Napaskiak, and the other half was baptized a year later. Then whenever an Orthodox priest visited he was welcomed to preach in the *kashgee,* until in 1935 a Russian Orthodox chapel was built. This may not mean that at any one point they had lost completely their indigenous mystique, but rather that they needed a new form in which to express their feelings. The mystery and color of Orthodox ceremony may have allowed a dynamic sublimation of Native spirit. Moravian Christianity, on the other extreme, meant strict rejection of all Eskimo ceremony.

Up the river from Bethel the nearest Eskimo village is Kwethluk, also a predominantly Orthodox community with an old Russian church. Kwethluk has a small Moravian church as well, and is just a few miles from the Moravian Children's Home which was established there in 1925. Both Kwethluk and Napaskiak are recognized for their order and self-determination.

The life style Oswalt observed in Napaskiak in 1955–56 revolved around Native subsistence of fishing, trapping, snaring, hunting, and berry picking. Ceremonialism surrounded these functional activities. The first game killed by a boy was celebrated with a feast that marked passage toward manhood. The first salmon a girl cleaned by herself was equally celebrated, as was her first pail of berries picked. The patterns of subsistence prescribed the Eskimo's day, season, and year, and created the Eskimo way. Hence survival of Eskimo ways had significant economic meaning. All the villages at this date shared these subsistent economic ties with their ecology. The villages remained dynamic centers; extensive family ties were functioning and important. Age roles from youth to manhood to old age were ordered and respected. Sex roles had changed because women held more recognized importance now that the home was the center rather than the *kashgee.* Villages with

Orthodox churches had a brilliant calendar of ceremonial events comparable to the indigenous calendar of ceremonials. Conceivably the villages that were predominantly Moravian may have changed psychically and spiritually toward a more individual destiny accomplished through the religious value attached to morality and hard work, but all acculturation was modified by the life style of Arctic existence.

Yet by the end of the 1960s, Eskimo life style was drastically transformed. Innovations entered Kuskokwim life that wrought more profound changes than all the years of Moravian teaching. Change came not through objective teaching but through accelerated diffusion of modern technological process and modern technological economy.

A similar transformation has taken place among the Hopi, Zuni, and other Indian villages in the Southwest with comparable historical circumstance. The Hopi, as one model, not very long ago had a delicately balanced subsistence of farming and stock raising, both of which succeeded or failed depending on rain. Rain for crops laid down the Hopi's total association with their world, and ceremonial and supernatural life revolved around moisture, fertility, and harvest. Hopi character and social structure were established around these realities.

The Hopi, too, were living in great isolation—of plateau desert instead of moist tundra. The Hopi lost their isolation through worldly education at boarding schools and later by traveling away from home to seek work, as well as by the accelerated

Home of the janitor of the BIA school in Tuluksak (upper income).

invasion of strangers. Finally roads penetrated the Hopi world so that the trading centers of Winslow and Flagstaff were only hours away. Diffusion of modern needs, washing machines, radios, and most expensively, pickup trucks, required cash. Hopi desert gardens cannot supply dollars. Fleece and lamb crops, like beaver and fox pelts, proved an unstable base because pasturage became over-grazed, drought decimated flocks, and the price of wool fluctuated for a host of reasons unrelated to grass or vagaries of rain. Today it can be safely said that no Hopi family makes its major subsistence from farming; someone in every family works for cash somewhere. Yet the social order and ceremonialism of Hopi remain remarkably stable, simply because they have replaced the subsistence functionalism of farming and dance prayer for moisture with new recognition of the need to retain their villages and go on being Hopi people. Hopi integrity had to find survival in the modern world.

The tundra Eskimos now face a similar challenge. White technology and White values have become rooted in Eskimo ways, and the subsistence economies of river and tundra no longer supply the trade value that can purchase White-type needs. In effect, Eskimo survival economy and the remote villages have become obsolete in modern eyes. The market for fur is unstable. The time it takes to trap fur is no longer expendable. A self-sufficient existence in nature becomes increasingly difficult.

Like the Hopi, the Eskimos live each year in less isolation. Outboard motors, motorized snowmobiles, and the constant roar of the bush planes have put the

remotest villages in close contact day after day with the modern world. Wage work has entered the Arctic in successive waves since the war with oil exploration and fish canneries. Building projects and national defense projects have employed whole villages and interrupted their ways of Arctic survival. This has happened less on the Kuskokwim than elsewhere in Alaska, but going away from the village to make cash is increasingly becoming an economic necessity. When the subsistence base of the village goes, the very survival of the village is shaken. Innovations of the last few years have radically altered the functions of the villages.

The war began the intrusions that place the villages in a precarious balance today. This balance has been tipped further by federal and state relief. This has struck at the economic heart of a frugal basically subsistence economy. Relief, old age pensions, Social Security, and unemployment insurance have filled the villages with a new source of cash usually with the stipulation that the recipient *not* be self-employed. The Post Office becomes the trap line. In 1969 in Tuluksak only one Eskimo ran a trap line, a man already employed as the VISTA worker's assistant. Various sources of relief shared around enough affluence so that the hardships of winter hunting and trapping were pragmatically unnecessary. Eskimos are very practical folk, and why go off into the frozen bush when you can just as productively socialize at home?

Significantly, this inertia does not affect summer fishing and hunting, which is for food rather than for cash. As soon as the ice begins to break in the rivers the Eskimo community awakes from the long social winter. Relief subsidies are forgotten. Steps quicken, smiles lengthen. Everyone is getting ready for the fishing, repairing canoes for muskrat hunting. Boats piled along the river are cleared of ice and trash, scraped and recalked. Outboard motors that have lain unattended in the snow all winter are broken down and lubricated. The village reaches an action pitch as the first boats are launched. And while ice pans still crowd the channel, Eskimos race their outboard-driven skiffs up and down the river to the rejoicing of the villagers who crowd forward to see the spring activity begin.

The introduction of the motorized snowmobiles in the late 1960s is another technological innovation that instantly affected the Eskimo ecology. Dog teams are created by nature, fed by nature, and are adaptive to the crises of the Arctic that threaten survival. Dogs can be the eyes and ears that save the traveler in the swirling blizzard. Indeed as a final resort, you can eat your dogs! But despite these advantages, dogs are a lot of trouble and eat a lot of fish both in summer and in winter.

Snowmobiles feed on imported gasoline only when they run, but they have no eyes and ears. They are very costly and have a short mechancial life. Worse, they can break down at the most critical time in Native eyes. Yet snowmobiles are White man's magic and the utilization of White man's power. An Eskimo has to have a Sno-Go just as a Hopi has to have a pickup truck. The technology involved is not entirely new. For years the river Eskimos have had outboard motors which greatly affected their salmon fishing and gave them great summer mobility for trading in Bethel. The Sno-Go gives them even greater mobility in winter. It requires no fish—which probably is affecting patterns of summer fishing, for dog teams have always been a major reason for smoking and storing fish. In a few years snowmobiles have phased out many dog teams. Now fishermen sometimes have a surplus of salmon, which can be consumed by the family as well as the dogs. Salmon is increasing as a commercial commodity and taking the place of furs as currency. If fishing were organized, salmon could become an economic mainstay, for the commercial demand for salmon may be far more stable than the market for fur.

How have the Hopi and other modern Indian groups survived the onslaught of change and needs that appear hostile to traditional cultural survival? In some fashion their sense of integrity has been gained by education, awareness, and sophistication. Can White schools help Eskimos into a self-determined future? Or is this an absurd notion? Is the realistic function of White studies to integrate Eskimos into the economic mainstream of American life? Does this automatically doom the villages? Or can Eskimos appraise their life style the way the Hopi have and reestablish themselves practically in modern Alaska? White educators in Alaska generally say the villages are doomed, but then outsiders may not be able to see any other function than profits made.

Boarding school education for countless village young people has already drained off much vitality. Eskimos have career jobs in Bethel in various state and federal agencies. Do they find fulfillment in Bethel or Anchorage? Saturday morning in the remotest Eskimo village is a roar of bush planes skimming down on the river ice. This is the return to the village from cash jobs in Bethel. Each weekend scores of single youths and young couples pay the $80 for a round-trip charter flight to spend two days in their village, to take a steam bath, to eat Eskimo food, to relax and socialize in the hospitality of the village.

Does this contemporary desire to return to the village describe new needs and fulfillment in Eskimo culture within the Arctic ecology? Is living successfully within the tundra environment essential to the fulfillment of many modern Eskimos as it was for Eskimos two or three generations ago?

The increase of White men in the Arctic indicates that the "good life" is there for modern man as it was for the indigenous hunter. What do Eskimos need to learn today to master the modern ecology if they wish to find their identity in their home land?

3 / Methodology of filming and analysis

WHY USE FILM?

Bethel is a hub of communication and transportation for planes that fly in by the hundreds from all points of the compass. Bush planes on skis roar off the river ice for the multitude of Eskimo villages—down on the Bering Sea, out on the vast tundra, and up and down the Kuskokwim and its winding tributaries. By summer the river is a highway for barges and outboard-driven fishing skiffs, by winter a frozen path for dog sleds, and increasingly the gasoline-driven snowmobile. All journeys begin and end on the frozen river front before the Northern Commercial Company post.

On my first day in Bethel I stood on the river piling and looked down on the snarling or sleeping sled dogs and now silent metallic Sno-Go's and tried to picture where these sleds and machines would be at their journey's end. In a very few days I too would be flying up river to begin filming Eskimo education. I would be working alone trying to record, often in one visit to an isolated tundra school, sufficient data to define the culture of each school and each class.

In two weeks the field team, John Connelly, Ray Barnhardt, his wife Carol, and their baby son John, would arrive for a two months residence. John, Ray, and Carol would meticulously study first, fifth, eight, ninth and tenth grades in the Bethel Consolidated School. They would execute "Draw-a-Man" tests and questionnaires and schedule interviewing with teachers, students, parents, and important village persons.

Six months earlier I had sat in Boulder, Colorado, with the leaders and regional fieldworkers of the National Study of American Indian Education. Each day for two weeks we gathered in seminars redesigning this verbal methodology, testing the questionnaires on each other and on Indians in the local Public Health hospital. What would be the returns of my colleagues using these most precise verbal recordings? What would my film data offer that this thoroughly programmed study would not gather?

First, we look at the returns of our colleagues, who make their statements mostly from the study of questionnaires and scheduled interviews. This brings in data on *one level,* and final interpretations rest on highly abstracted evidence, the speculative verbal state—speculative, because words *are* abstract mind signals that are recovered within a wide range of meaning, first within the Native's response and later in a researcher's interpretation. The data must be seen always over a communication chasm of *words*.

Film documentation is nonverbal, hence at many points less speculative and more open to critical judgment by a team of analysts. It is, in this sense, a very low level of documentary abstraction that is as sensual as it is intellectual, and therefore offers the analyst emotional-psychological opportunities difficult to research from verbal projections.

But why not still-photographic recording, which would be both cheaper and less cumbersome within the field circumstance?

Fifteen years of experiement have fixed reasonable limits of still-photographic evidence. The still camera does a fine job of inventorying what is there. It counts and measures responsibly. But it has serious limitations when *motion* is of a major research importance. True, one *can* make voluminous time-and-motion scheduled, still-photographic studies, but both making and analyzing these studies become extremely awkward and more time consuming than the film record. Time-and-motion records of the still camera are fixed points of human phenomena. Projectively the *mind* must link behavior together between these fixed points. The result tends to be a gross assumption or to be impressionistic in judgment. Film *flows* photographically and *links* all time stations without impressionism, and therefore allows for authentic observation of *motion*.

My colleagues in the National Study were getting the fixed facts. We hoped film would offer the emotional flow between facts and allow us to discuss genuinely the emotional-psychological behavior of the child in education. The decision to research with film was based on advanced studies by anthropologists and psychologists concerned with nonverbal behavior. We thank pioneers in visual anthropology for much of our methodology. Edward T. Hall formally introduced us to the cultural opportunities of film analysis. He demonstrated vividly on film with slow-motion projection of three culturally different groups of people at a fiesta—Indians, Spanish-Americans, and Anglos—how each moved consistently within a program of behavior which was totally synchronized within each group. Could we make a similar record in classrooms and thereby describe school culture from nonverbal behavior?

Paul Byers of Columbia has also carried nonverbal recordings into analysis of group behavior. Byers has demonstrated that people in any cultural circumstance are consistently programmed in their use of space and body expression (Mead, Byers, 1967).

We have used Hall's concept of *proxemics,* space in culture, and we have been constantly grateful to Ray Birdwhistell (1969) for his studies in *kinesics,* the significance of body posture. Birdwhistell analyzed two minutes of film made by Gregory Bateson of a disturbed mother and child, and through kinesics was able to diagnose accurately a state of psychiatric stress. Film appears able to document emotional stress and well-being, and this opportunity has been a major objective in our research.

Paul Ekman, in association with Langley Porter Clinic in San Francisco, has also carried out many years of study in psychiatric nonverbal behavior and stabilized film reading to a point where Langley Porter can use film responsibly in diagnosis.

Finally, as is inevitable in visual anthropology, we are indebted to Margaret Mead and Gregory Bateson for laying the cornerstones that have made the studies of nonverbal behavior a reality in anthropolgy. *Business Character: A Photographic Analysis* (1842) offered many clues to making and analyzing our film research.

WHAT WE WERE LOOKING FOR

Our study was focused on schools, wherever Eskimo children received an education. In the problem of educating Native children, were particular school systems experiencing more difficulties and negative results than others? We were particularly interested in BIA schools because historically they have set the style of Indian education. However, the quality of BIA schools may be considerably less crucial an issue than it used to be, simply because more Indian and Eskimo students are attending state and public schools than federal schools today, and the field of Native education has thereby left the remote reservation for the congested cities.

Beyond the question of the character of Native schools, the film study was attempting to chart the human and educational behavior of Eskimo children on three curves: an ecological-geographic curve, a cultural-ethnic distribution curve, and an age cycle curve.

Ranging from the remote Eskimo village, to the larger more progressive village, to the tundra city salmon fishing center, and finally to the modern White city of Anchorage, our film sample allowed the camera to watch the relative learning pace of the children as it changed, from the most undisturbed environment to the most impersonal, un-Eskimo environment available in Alaska. Does school setting affect learning and emotional well-being? Are teachers less or more responsive to students' welfare as Eskimos in tiny village schools as compared to the city school environment in Anchorage? Are changes of concern related to how teachers teach and how students learn? Is there real value in making sacrifices to teach in remote villages? Or is it educationally more successful to move Eskimo children into large centers with greater interaction and fuller educational advantages? Is environmental and cultural security really significant in Native education?

The second curve followed the range of Eskimo children's response to the ethnic composition of the classroom, from the totally Eskimo schools in the villages to the predominantly Eskimo student body in Bethel where 85 percent of the school children are Eskimo, and finally to the predominantly White schools in Anchorage, where only 7 percent of the students are Native—Indians, Eskimos, and Aleuts. Is there a relationship between well-being and the ethnic composition of the classroom? Do Eskimos respond better within their own group? How do they respond as a small minority in the genuinely desegregated school? This insight might be very important in discussing the value of BIA education versus public school attendance. Should Natives near White communities be bussed out of their village schools into the stimulation of White schools? Or is the concept of the village ethnic community school one key to effective education for Native children? Is there a relationship to the school dropout rate in this ethnic distribution curve?

The third curve was the age cycle. The class sample of the National Study included first, second, fifth, eighth, and tenth grades. To correlate with their work, I covered the same sample of classes, but broadened this coverage to include early childhood education as well—Head Start, kindergarten, and pre-first—and special education classes, all of which we felt were very important in considering Indian education. Thus the age curve ranged from Head Start to tenth grade, or from about 4 to 16 or 17 years old. Where on this curve do Eskimo children exhibit the most intensity in learning? Is there an age or grade at which children begin to show signs of alienation or stress? If the students exhibit stress at adolescence, is this essentially physiological? Or is this tress also environmentally related? In the background of this query is, of course, the historical debate over ethnically segregated schools versus integrated schools.

Questions were also asked as to the value of Natively relevant material in the curriculum, the value of bilingualism, and the possible educational empathy of Native teachers versus Caucasian teachers. Since the film sample included a few instances of these elements, I have also evaluated, on a very small sample, the effect of relevant curriculum and the resourcefulness of Native teachers in terms of relevance and communication.

The filming was designed to gather samples systematically, class to class and school to school, so that later we could search for the same behavior variables and produce findings that would represent the impact and significance of twenty hours of classroom experience. The combined evidence will support observations of the *goals* of Eskimo education and the character of educational programming for Eskimo children.

TECHNICAL CONSIDERATIONS

How to make this film record? Should I use conventional 16mm film? Or should I use Super 8mm film, which is considered an amateur medium? This question was answered immediately by the budget. To achieve relevance would require many hours of film. Sixteen-millimeter would skyrocket the cost of the research. The Super 8 image is satisfactorily sharp. The cost of a Super 8 camera that would allow us to make time lapse studies was relatively low. So was the cost of a projector designed to study time lapse frame for frame (the Eastman Ektomatic Super 8 projector). Also, processing costs thousands of dollars in 16 mm. In many ways it was a hard photographic decision to make, for almost surely it would limit our film to research only; to date it is extremely difficult to produce audience film with Super 8. But audience use of film was no issue in this study as the intimacy of these recordings would ethically ban public distribution.

The next decision was how much to film. Considering the breadth of our sample we budgeted three rolls per class, two rolls at the conventional eighteen frames per second and one roll at automatic time lapse at two frames per second. This offered two varieties of recovery. The first was about nine minutes of film time devoted to long sequences following both general and specific activities, usually shot within a half hour. The second was a systematic exaggeration of body motion that made behavior patterns easy to see. Two frames per second, projected at four or six frames per second, literally dissects body expression. Time lapse also allows for rapid frame-for-frame analysis for refined measure of kinesic, proxemic, and time factors.

Ideally, I chose a location where all of the students and teachers were in view. The camera was usually on a tripod, and before filming there was a time period allowed for teacher and students to adjust to the presence of a camera. Usually halfway through the filming the camera could be removed from the tripod and I could wander about the room when relevant material was not clearly seen from the initial position. The camera had a zoom lens so that individual behavior could be filmed intimately without moving the camera. Slow pans were used to keep in track all behavior in the class.

After the filming, an inventory of classrooms was made with the 35mm still camera. Still records can document detail of walls and teaching materials with more precision than the moving picture camera and offer an easier analysis opportunity than film.

The final decision of technique was in relation to sound recording. Lip synchronization was technically, as well as financially, out of the question. It would have required many thousands of dollars' worth of equipment and the constant presence of a sound technician. But sound recorded simultaneously for content was thoroughly practical. Therefore every class filmed was sound logged with a SONY tape recorder. This was the only documentary way that behavior and curriculum could be correlated. Also, the noise level could be related to teaching method. The recorder was left in a central position in the class and allowed to run through the entire time involved in the filming.

READING THE EDUCATIONAL EVIDENCE ON FILM

How were we to analyze twenty hours of film? Frame-for-frame study on the order of Birdwhistell's and Ekman's work could take four years. Instead we had to design a study of controlled judgments by a team of trained observers. Slow motion and frame-for-frame relationships could be afforded only at key points of significance.

Members of the team had all studied or were studying visual anthropology and shared a background of crosscultural understanding. Alyce Cathey, a Eurasian with several years teaching experience, was currently teaching English as a second language to Chinese children in San Francisco. Paul Michaels, a master's candidate in education, had taught several years in Head Start, including one year in northwestern Alaska. Mack Ford was a master's candidate in anthropology with research experience in education and photography. Malcolm Collier was an anthropology major with years of life among indigenous people and experience as a photographer.

To synchronize our analyses we found it essential to state explicitly how education could be seen on film. Preliminary study indicated that *communication* is vividly apparent in the classes that the judges felt were educationally alive. Minus and plus qualities in communication appeared the most significant factors. We found it important to agree on one major assumption to simplify the tremendous overload invariably present in the photographic document and help us develop a view that would lead to an agreed conclusion.

> *Assumption*:   Education is a *communication* process—from teacher to student, from student to teacher, between student and student, *and between the student and himself.*
> *Corollary*:   From viewing film *we cannot tell whether education is taking place*, but we might be able to tell circumstantially *if* education *could take place*, and be reasonably sure of the circumstances in which education *is not taking place.*

(An analogy of the visible proof within the model: If telephone wires are seen entering a house we can assume that messages *might* be sent or received; if telephone wires are dangling, unattached to the house, we can safely assume there is no longer telephone communication.)

We studied our footage as *film,* only occasionally studying behavior frame for frame. Hence our variables primarily are in motion, and much of our qualified observation was seen in the sequence of time. Thus time itself was a variable.

We tried to standardize nonverbal communication patterns so that we could recognize behavioral elements in a comparable way. The basic elements for nonverbal research in still images are very similar to those in film, though film offers special subtleties visible only *in* film. These tangible elements are of three dimensions:

Birdwhistell's *Kinesics*—the language of posture and gesture

Hall's *Proxemics*—the language of space

Flow of time as a measure of duration of human performance and the validity of behavior seen only through repetition in time.

A fourth element is the comparability *between* classrooms, which offers a most important descriptive opportunity. Indeed without the element of contrast and comparison between classes the first three elements have only limited usefulness. Comparison of a large number of differing classes was the core of the analysis of the film data.

Examples of Communication in the Classroom

1) TEACHER SENDING:
   Kinesics: Gestures of message projection
   Eye messages, hand messages, body posture messages
   Visual display of artifacts that communicate
   Proxemics: Space between teacher and student as a communication variable
   Space adjustment as an effort in communication
   Extreme proximity for one-to-one projection
   Touching the listener, body-to-body communication
   STUDENT RECEIVING:
   Kinesics: Eye reception, attention, focus
   Body reception—turning toward sender, leaning toward sender
   Proxemics: Space adjustment to improve reception
   Touching the teacher for body-to-body reception
   Time: Internalization span of listening
   Ability over a time span to reject interruptions and distractions

In the BIA school in Kwethluk students often sit in straight lines. Film clip records the effort of pre-first students to "Stay in your seats!" in a straight line of chairs. We can observe they are not physically relating and form a distracted group. Compare with film clip of Head Start class, p. 79.

2) STUDENT SENDING:
Kinesics: Signalling to teacher
                   Hands up; eye signals, speech signals, body signals
Proxemics: Adjustment of space for better projection
                   Communication by touch
Time: Measure of time span of communication

TEACHER RECEIVING:
Kinesics: Response by eye reception
                   Leaning forward to listen
                   Body reception—nodding, head-shaking, hand signal an-
                   swers
Proxemics: Adjustment in space to hear better
                   Reception by body touch
Time: Measure of listening span of teacher

3) STUDENT TO STUDENT COMMUNICATION:
Kinesics: Eye focus for projection and reception
                   Hand messages, approval, disapproval, etc.
                   Collaborative reception during lesson or over assignments
Proxemics: Body proximity and body touch signaling
                   Passing notes, holding out books or other lesson objects
                   Extra-curricular communication, object sharing, joint ac-
                   tivities that link together a peer culture

4) STUDENT TO SELF COMMUNICATION:
Programming: Social freedom in the classroom that allows the student to
                   withdraw and think through his own problems and do
                   self-directed study
Proxemics: Student operating in his own air space even within con-
                   gested classroom
                   Images of inner-directed concentration in the classroom
Time: Measure of time freedom offered each student to work out
                   his own problem or complete his own creative work

5) VARIABLES OF MOTIVATION OR BOREDOM:
Positive: Coordinated body posture, responding to communication
                   stimulus
                   Eye behavior suggesting focus of attention
                   Face signaling expectation and concentration, tonal char-
                   acter of facial muscles
                   Hand signals of cognition
Negative: Body coordination directed away from stimulus of communi-
                   cation
                   Body tonus slack and uncoordinated, slouched
                   Eye behavior suggesting near sleep, daydreaming, out the
                   window
                   Facial muscles slack and uncoordinated by lack of intel-
                   lectual or emotional focus

6) EMOTIONAL WELL-BEING OR STRESS:
Well-being: Physical stance of confidence and command over classroom
                   circumstance
                   Stance suggesting confidence and command over personality
                   Body behavior suggesting flow of physical and emotional
                   energy
                   Eye response and body reactions revealing alertness

Facial and body signals of peaceful adjustment to circumstance and pleasure gained from classroom environment

Stress: Body tension suggesting fear, withdrawal from classroom
interaction, inability to communicate

Withdrawal suggested by body slumping, head pillowed on
arms, etc.

Facial expression of stress, knitted brows, tense lips, suggesting fear, hostility, or resentment

With all these considerations in mind each team member studied every foot of
classroom film and logged observations on a scheduled analysis sheet including:

General impression of class
Asthetic look and tone of the classroom, physical layout
Relationships between staff and child
Relationships between child and child
Relationships between child and staff
Character of these communicational situations: verbal/non-verbal
Is the teacher oriented toward individuals or toward the group?

These scheduled observations were inventories of *what is there* in terms of visible
evidence and allowed us to track systematically the imagery to describe the general
shape and effect of Eskimo education.

The researchers worked alone, each viewing all the footage and listening to the
tapes. The film was looked at without stopping, stopped, run slow-motion, and
clicked through frame for frame for spot analysis of refinement of behavior. In
addition to the schedule of observation, each member wrote his own general evaluation, class for class. The consensus was fairly even, and where there were discrepancies, these classes were restudied.

After the initial film reading was completed, these data sheets were coded and
the material transferred to key-punch cards which carried our study to a further
abstraction that defined the educational movement from the tundra villages to
Bethel and finally to the city of Anchorage.

How did the sound recording figure in our evaluations?

Because we are a verbally-oriented people, the team found that if the tapes
were played with the film, the verbal stimuli drained off the nonverbal sensitivity
and made visual reading difficult. Hence a large part of the film analysis was done
with silent film. The tapes, on the other hand, when played as a check against the
silent reading of the film, often deepened and gave substance to the judgment of
the classrooms. In effect the tapes were *explanatory* but did not prove revealing in
themselves.

As author of the report, I studied all the team's observations, listened to the
tapes, and rescreened every film. I would move from projector to typewriter and
montage the joint observations on all the classrooms. Chapter 5, "The classrooms
on film," is this combined statement. Throughout the research I leaned confidently
on the most rewarding character of photographic data, the analyst's opportunity
to go back again and again to the undisturbed raw data. Despite intrusions of sub-
jectivity that invades even the technology of photography, I believe the photographic record remains the most undistorted evidence we have of human behavior.

4 / Observations on the field experience

THE PHOTOGRAPHER AS PARTICIPANT OBSERVER

The *act* of taking pictures is a complete experience in itself, just as the making of a survey, apart from its data, reveals many aspects of the field circumstance.

My first impression was that teachers and principals are much more prepared to answer questions than to appear before the camera. The verbal examination can be more controlled and directed by the informant toward a desired impression. Question answering is often from an armored position and therefore tolerable.

The nonverbal examination is harder to control, especially if it goes on continuously. Hence schools are at first agitated over the request to film them. "Why?," "What for?," "Who will see the film?" are immediate queries that must be answered. But once such hurdles had been crossed, 90 percent of the teachers were relaxed and pretty much ignored my presence in their rooms. I am not saying they *forgot* that I was there. Rather, each teacher is so programmed in behavior that during an hour's visit it seemed difficult, or even psychologically impossible, to change his pattern fundamentally. Hence poor teachers continued on their negative programs, and good teachers continued turning students on in a relaxed way that made me feel unseen.

Every student seemed familiar with photography and film, and they often showed a keen interest in the process. They were allowed to look through the camera and to ask questions. But they, too, settled rapidly into an established classroom pattern of being teacher-bored, sleepy, distracted, or interacting with excitement to the lesson. My presence in all but a few cases seemed neither to add nor to distract. Maybe this is a quality of film, for it flows on with time, on the same time river that is carrying the students to freedom at the class's end. The still camera takes a slice *out* of time, and can both interrupt and distort behavior for this reason.

Working through the superintendent of the State of Alaska's Consolidated Elementary and High School in the tundra city of Bethel was a very different circumstance from visiting isolated BIA village schools. The state school superintendent was verbally concerned about how his teachers would respond to the filming, but bureaucratically he was in control of their cooperation, and with varying degrees of interest the teachers dutifully collaborated.

To work in the village school was at the prerogative of the Bureau of Indian

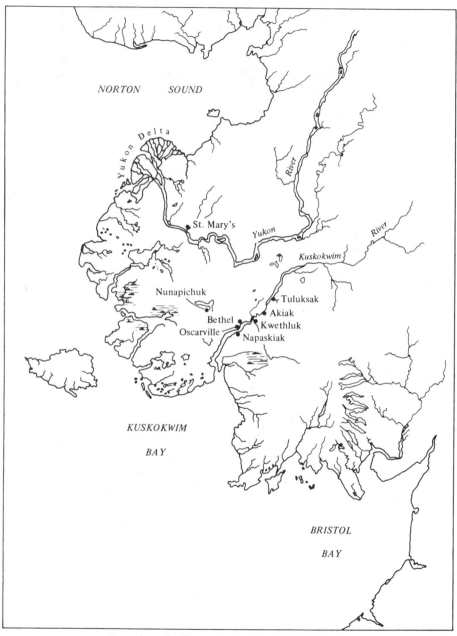

Location of villages in the Kuskokwim Basin.

Affairs' director of education for the Kuskokwim schools. In some ways my request for film observation was more threatening to the BIA than to the state school system. Once the Bethel superintendent adjusted to my presence and to the observations of Connelly and the Barnhardts, he was enthusiastically opportunistic, for he recognized that we wished a complete and honest picture that might realistically benefit the school. After a month he saw us, in a sense, as collaborators rather than as spies. The state school system is expanding rapidly in Alaska and is success-oriented. The BIA school system is shrinking, is under attack, and therefore is extremely sensitive to any observation.

A major anxiety suggested by the BIA superintendent as to why filming would be difficult was the predictable tension in the isolated schools. I was told that the teachers did not welcome visitors (contrary to the human assumption that they would like a break in their monotony) and that they were usually too harassed and busy with school affairs to be able to work with a visitor. I was given the impression that thousands of miles out on the tundra wastes teachers were harassed by hostile or wasteful studies, and therefore not always hospitable. Further, and of course logically, there simply were no accommodations except in the teachers' own homes. Indeed, everything is short in the wilderness. Supplies of all kinds must be purchased a year ahead. Because teachers are apparently besieged with senators and educators making surveys, the usual Anchorage prices should be paid for hospitality—$15 a night and $3 a meal were permissible prices for visiting observers. Yet each teacher accommodated visitors on his own terms—humanly established between teacher and fieldworker.

The area director was sincerely concerned about the psychological welfare of his field staff. Talking things over in a cement radar personnel site converted to a BIA nerve center of welfare and education, I got the message that life in the remote village school was a hazardous assignment and the turnover of personnel high. Nothing must happen that would upset the precarious equilibrium of the isolated teachers. I left by bush plane for the villages with the feeling that I was entering an explosive assignment.

ISOLATION AND SURVIVAL CULTURE

The Kuskokwim Basin in winter appears as coils of frozen waterways and lakes fringed with stunted black spruce and willows. In the southeast there are glistening mountains, but west and north the tundra wastes slope to the horizon. In this vastness, a village is sighted close to waterways—a scattering of cabins, a shimmering metallic school compound, a National Guard Quonset hut. Villages can be 15, 30, or 40 air-minutes from Bethel, 8 hours or 24 hours by dog sled, 2 or 4 hours by gasoline-driven snowmobile.

Villages range in size from 50 to 250 Eskimos, who only a few years ago lived off the wilderness—salmon fishing and berry picking in summer; rabbit snaring, deer, elk, and moose hunting, and fur trapping in winter. The salmon still remain a major foundation, but old-age pensions, relief, and National Guard stipends have become the economic way of life, especially through the long winters. Every year

Home of a middle income family in Tuluksak.

fewer Eskimos endure the rigors of the winter hunting camps and beaver trap lines.

As the bush plane skims over the river ice low between river banks, one's first impression is that public health has come to the Arctic, for the most imposing structures are the multitudes of neatly painted white outhouses. The second impression is of the barking sled dogs staked out by the privies and then of the Eskimos who gather to watch the mail plane skid to a halt below the diminutive village post office. The mail sled skids down the bank, pushed by laughing children followed by elders, some dressed in Army high-altitude flying gear, others in traditional wolf-fringed parkas. The Eskimos like visitors. They are amused and curious about strangers and eager to make them welcome—a normal response, we humanly assume, to life in great isolation. Travelers have always agreed that Eskimos are very sociable folk.

I have observed, on the contrary, that White people of status (and most White people come with status) dropped on contract assignments into the moist, green isolation of tropical jungles or dropped into the white isolation of the Arctic, often respond to the circumstance by creating further isolation by walling themselves off both from the ecology and from the Native humanity around them.

White schoolteachers in Native schools face this dilemma. Some of the walls that rise around them are self-fulfilling conflicts of culture, strengthened by the bureaucratic and technological zeal of a government agency. By White standards Eskimo villages are pitifully poor, unhygienic, and shockingly overcrowded, often with two families jammed into one small log cabin 15 feet by 25. As in any

60

School teachers' home in the BIA school compound in Tuluksak.

survival economy, per capita income would be far below even the conventional poverty line if relief and government succor were removed.

Abruptly, in the midst of all this apparent squalor and staked-out sled dogs stands the BIA school compound. Its life pulse is its diesel light plant, which makes the compound a mecca of blazing illumination in the darkness of the village. (Two villages now have their own light plants.) By day the BIA buildings shimmer in aluminum and fresh paint. Nothing has been spared to make these units ideal models of White mastery, technology, and comfort. On the one hand, the excellence of the buildings speaks for the drive of the curriculum; on the other, the technology and comforts are essential for the emotional well-being of the staff. The comfortable life style of the teachers' home culture is imported, indeed refined upon, to make life tolerable in the Arctic isolation.

I am sure these comforts do make life tolerable on one level, but on another they greatly increase the isolation. Teachers exist within this comfort style and rarely go outside its walls—except to hunt, which is the one ecologically oriented outlet for male teachers in the villages.

To live within such small space requires great skills in self-fulfillment and high tolerance to human shortcomings. The shock of the circumstance, too, often weakens both these skills. Marriages crack, and contracts are broken. The one skill that most field personnel develop highly is the skill of keeping busy. Fortunately the bureaucracy of the BIA cooperates in this, for if all the forms and receipts are filled out regularly, if radio communications are kept and duly logged, there is literally little time for any other activity. But the busy-ness becomes another wall of isolation not only from the community and the ecology but also from wanting to have visitors observing their operations. Indeed, once inside the educational compound, it is difficult to set up after-school interviews with teachers; they are too busy or they are exhuasted.

Behind this inaccessibility there are, of course, other real challenges of individual survival. Quite realistically, to keep air space and peace within the limited and nigh impenetrable walls of the compound (winter temperatures hover for days at 50 below zero), personal privacy must be religiously respected. Under the stress and multiple culture shock, holding together as a person in this isolation is indeed a challenge. Too often self-survival is sought with introversion and further imposed isolations that resent the arrival of strangers.

Well-being anywhere is obtained in a complex scheme of resources. When Eskimos move to San Francisco, this struggle for adjustment can be viewed in reverse. One Eskimo we observed in Oakland was unable to transplant himself. He worked, came home, sat in a compulsively neat but empty house, with no ties with the surrounding community, and drank himself into a psychiatric disaster that required that he be shipped back to the Arctic. Clearly the success of such transplants depends on the ability to transport sufficient life style so that minimal well-being can be retained. When a familiar diet is broken and new foods rejected, a "crack-up" in personality can take place. For most teachers a contract in the Arctic is an abrupt interruption of normal life that will not begin again until they return to the "Lower Forty-Eight." This is as true among teachers in the state system at Bethel as in the village schools of the BIA. Busy-ness is an anesthetic that certainly helps many through the Arctic winter. But this tends to be a frantic solution unless other outlets and relationships are achieved.

RELATING TO THE ARCTIC

The primary basis on which many·teachers relate to the Arctic is linked to their reason for deciding to come to work with the Eskimos in the first place. Some come for adventure, but others come out of a real concern for the advertised deprivation of the Eskimo. The well-fed hold out a hand to the hungry. Modern man brings aid to primitive peoples—a missionary zeal that contains empathy but also a severe sense of inequality. They come north to *help* the Eskimo. Few come north to *learn*. And, too, many others come north for the money. Again, this is a general view of White teachers in the Arctic.

The motivated teachers of Eskimos approach their tasks with enthusiasm. But as the year passes, enthusiasm may too often change to a fatalism about the hopelessness of the task of educating the Eskimo within his life and habitat. For many the very cultural style of their students' families is a block against education. Villagers can appear to lack progressive motivation. Indeed, Eskimos can appear lazy and improvident because they often do not find White goals of much value. For too many motivated teachers the year's contract ends in negative discouragement.

The adventure-oriented teacher, usually male, often does relate to Eskimo survival skills in hunting and fishing. Alaska is a man's world, and though sports-oriented teachers retain well-being, their solution is usually outside the village and does not necessarily direct their teaching. Nor does it occur to them to adjust school-attendance scheduling so that Eskimo children could learn these skills also. Other Arctic-oriented teachers become collectors—Eskimo masks, *mukluks,* valuable furs, and exquisite parkas. But this interest in Eskimo artifacts, again, does not necessarily reach out to the Eskimo villagers or weave into classroom activity in terms of a culturally involved curriculum.

The few career teachers who stay for many years in the Arctic are the exception. For these unusual people school busy-ness may be replaced by deeper involvements. Real friendships are formed in the villages. Individual teachers in the past have been very influential in developing cooperatives and starting light plants in the villages. These lasting teachers are not so driven. On film they appear relaxed and generally live a human leisurely pattern.

One such teacher is a pilot, owns his own plane, and visits up and down the Kuskokwim. His wife is adept in first aid and generously directs an Eskimo village health worker. A circumstance that may be a key to their "lasting" is their philosophical view of their jobs. Generally they keep educational goals low, or "real," in keeping with their aspirations for the Eskimo villagers. This view can become a fatalism, reinforced by years of experience, that closes the door on radical innovation. This philosophical view allows them genuinely to like the Eskimos, but at the same time precludes their envisioning anything but a limited horizon for these villagers unless they leave. These teachers have another great value: they stay, which is in itself educational. They have been a stimulation to students to reach the goals *they* feel are practical and progressive for the Eskimo. But it is precisely because of goals of this nature that American Indian education is now under grave question.

These observations are not directed solely toward a special BIA culture, but as stated earlier, toward White people contracted to work in wilderness isolation. The State of Alaska is taking more and more of the schools over from the BIA, and it is hard to imagine that circumstances would be radically different for state teachers. Basically I am describing the teacher environment of isolated Eskimo schools taught by culturally different White teachers. My observations are directed toward how this compound culture affects education. Furthermore, I am not describing a situation that is wholly predestined and not subject to change; indeed if it were, the substance of this report would be futile.

ESKIMO CHILDREN

Eskimo children must be the most rewarding kids in the world to teach. This is one's immediate response to any Eskimo classroom in an isolated village. There is enough Eskimo life style left to retain the traditional personality. Will this change if the survival culture of the Arctic environment is radically eroded by intrusive technology and dollars for work unrelated to the ecology? As of now, the Eskimo children are remarkably stable and optimistic, eager for innovation and knowledge of the world.

One rarely meets dour looks or difficult dispositions in the elementary grades.

Poor teaching skills and dull curriculum are yet not enough to dampen their spontaneity. They are apparently easy to lead and very cooperative. We have records of teachers who have capitalized on this opportunity; but in general, teachers in the villages make instruction hard work, apply themselves with compulsive intensity, and appear exhausted after a class period. You sense how hard it is for them to reach over to the Eskimo children from their own isolation. They appeared to be shouting lessons over a great gulf—and in the film there was considerable air distance as well as emotional distance between teachers and pupils.

Generally instruction was highly verbal with little feedback from the students. They sat dutifully in class, amazingly intent upon the teachers' words or else quietly squirming, yawning, and stretching. Was this because of a language block? Was their English even more limited than the teachers realized? Would they have communicated in Eskimo? Or did the teaching style limit verbal feedback?

SCHOOLS AND VILLAGES

The Bureau of Indian Affairs Compound

The total presence of the BIA school—its compound, staff, and technology—provides its educational impact on the village. As observed, the school plant is a model of White perfection which constantly contrasts with the tattered and weather-beaten Eskimo habitations. Each school has its maintenance workshop and ultramodern diesel light plant that runs continuously. Each school has a kitchen and a multipurpose room where hot lunches are served or bingo games held for the village on special evenings. The kitchen staff members wear uniforms and waitress-type hats and observe ultrahygienic routines.

The children's lives are spent running to the brightly lighted, windowed school with all its technology, and back home again over the snow or mud to small, dark, not too hygienic Native homes.

The educational staff of the village school is not limited to White teachers. Each school has an Eskimo teacher's aide and one, or sometimes as many as three, Eskimo maintenance and janitorial assistants, and an Eskimo kitchen staff. The Native staff members are elite villagers, skilled in White ways and considered intelligent and dependable. Also these Eskimo staff jobs may be the few cash opportunities available in the village and give the holders high status roles in the community.

The educational role of the teacher's aide is clear. Occasionally she sits down with a group of children in the lower grades and corrects their spelling or math. A lot of the time she stands, far away from the teacher, and waits for an order or a chance to be of service—finding the pointer, the chalk, the blackboard eraser, or handing out dittoed forms to students. Even in these modest services I am sure these aides are invaluable, if only for their ability to put the children at ease in Eskimo. What other educational functions these young women could be put to is a question to be examined later in our text.

The educational role of the various male Eskimo assistants is considerably more vague. Whatever their influence is, it is benign and most informal. As stated, they are highly selected personnel, educated in technology and adequate, if not fluent, in reading and writing. They are usually village leaders and belong to the National Guard. Could they be used to teach industrial arts and practical education and to be rewarding adult figures of educational success? In a related way, what further educational role could the kitchen staff offer the school?

A Village OEO Head Start

In the village of Kwethluk, a few hundred yards from the BIA compound, there is a contrasting school culture, the Head Start program financed by the Office of Economic Opportunity. For the Eskimos *this* is the village school, and the BIA is the government school.

The village Head Start class is held in the commodious planked council chamber of the village, and every service of this school is carried out *by* the village, including the instruction. Two young women of the village with BIA high school education and a summer's workshop in Fairbanks teach 5-year-old Eskimo children the rudiments of Mother Goose, English, and alphabet recognition. I suspect the class is far ahead of where early childhood education is supposed to be, but this village school is taught by alert and ambitious Eskimo women with a high regard for their pupils.

The OEO Head Start program is directed from Bethel by a traveling director, herself an Eskimo from this very village, who flies a circuit of village schools 80 miles in all directions from Bethel. Most of the time the young teachers are on their own, and so the school operates on its own level.

The principal at the neighboring BIA school was suspicious that all they did was in Eskimo, but when I played him a tape from Head Start he was amazed and impressed by the school's effectiveness in teaching English.

Viewed on film the school is *very* different from the BIA, and it is clear why this school made such progress. In the BIA prefirst as well as in the kindergarten at Bethel, there is a great deal of space between pupils and teachers. In this Head Start class, communication is body to body, and there is a current of communication running from teacher to students and back to teacher. The effect of this communication is clearly seen on film.

The BIA teachers are White and come and go. The Head Start teachers are kin to most of the children. Though English is used heavily in Head Start, it is easy to lapse into Eskimo whenever appropriate. This Head Start class was our one model of the effectiveness of Native teachers with minimal teacher training. This circumstance will be examined again in our conclusions.

A Moravian Mission Home and School

A variation from the school compound culture was the world of the Moravian Children's Home three miles from Kwethluk. The Home was established originally to accommodate Eskimo children from families stricken by tuberculosis. Now that TB is no longer the scourge that it was, the Home is for any child who needs care and education. A church and three commodious two-story lodges are strung through a clearing in the stunted spruce on a bend of a tributary of the Kuskokwim.

Through the summer, boats and barges stop at the Home, while in winter, planes land on the ice, and dog sled and Sno-Go link the Home with the post office downstream in Kwethluk.

Isolation is nearly complete, except for daily contact with the Home's Eskimo population. Here there is no village nor any opportunity to interact with the ecology except to be surrounded by it. Whereas in the villages the school hours tend to be culturally separated from Native life, here you find the school one large family with intense interaction between everyone around the clock.

The missionary commitment of Moravian personnel makes for continuity. It is a way of life, and many stay to retirement. The religious activity largely takes care of well-being and insists on at least an outwardly loving social relationship. As a missionary center, both the Children's Home and school are relaxed. The children seem spontaneously happy, and most of the human problems met in the compounds are solved by the Moravian culture of the Home. I am sure not all missionary schools achieve this relative harmony, and it is a question just what this Home offers in functioning education for Eskimos.

There is no overt culture conflict simply because the children are lifted totally from their own culture and submerged in the school. The extreme isolation makes everyone functionally dependent on everyone else. By comparison the BIA schools are in the mainstream of Arctic travel. Mail planes stop twice a week, and all day long bush planes are roaring in and out. The daily radio "skid" from Bethel holds each school in the bureaucracy. But the Moravian Home is "unto itself."

Compared to the BIA schools, education at the Home is limited to the three R's and vocational training such as typing. The plant is poor but stable, unequipped but severely thorough.

The school appeared to welcome visitors, and the director was eager to talk over the psychological problems of its charges. The question arises: Can such a mission school innovate to the bicultural needs of its students? Moravian missionaries initially took a very hostile view of Eskimo culture, and the summer school for Eskimo village lay readers still instructs against Eskimo culture in the form of dancing or traditional social life. Religious attendance in one village was fanatically compulsive, and the church program appeared not to concern itself with the survival problems of the community, such as building a cooperative, encouraging Arctic skill, and so on. One gets the impression that even here in the human warmth of the Home, orientation is *out* of the Arctic. The general education offered is in conflict with the life style of even the contemporary Eskimo. Looking out from the Home, the villages hardly exist. On the other hand, Bethlehem, Pennsylvania, seat of the Moravian church, is critically in focus.

THE TUNDRA CITY OF BETHEL

What kind of education do Eskimos receive from this busy hub of the Arctic? The school in Bethel is excellent as measured in White values—as are the BIA village schools, as well. But here the school is an appendage of the city, Bethel.

Bethel as a school for Eskimos might be compared to Gallup, N.M., as a school far Navajos. A liquor store pays the town's upkeep. And even though almost everyone agrees that this one liquor store is the scourge of all Eskimos living in or visiting Bethel, in the last election the store was voted permanence—for it *pays*. Some years earlier it had been voted closed, with a sigh of relief, but the loss of revenue was too severe. Beyond the liquor store are three richly stocked general stores to tempt the Eskimo further in his tastes for conspicuous consumption, as well as waste.

Bethel has a genuine slum, poor as shoddy cabins only can be when shadowed by affluence. So in one sense Bethel is the *world* that the White man's education is selling to the Eskimo. And as a world it has most of the White man's failures. Bethel could be looked upon as a proving ground for coping with White ways and perversities. Hence it *could* be a very educational spot.

The Alaska State School in Bethel holds itself aloof (as do most schools) from the larger classroom, the city, even though its superintendent is aware and resentful of that fact. Education in the Bethel School cannot be judged by such extreme standards, but considering how intimate Bethel community problems are to the school, education could do far more than it is doing for improvement of community life. It should be judged on how well it prepares and encourages Eskimos to deal with their immediate social and economic circumstances. This writing will examine some of these educational goals further on in the text.

Eskimos themselves may be using Bethel at large as a school far more effectively than they use the state school. Bethel is the site of the most militant co-op and the center for the most politically determined Eskimo group in the tundra. Villagers from nearby Nunapitchuk form the backbone of the salmon cooperative based in Bethel and are the leading group in the Alaskan Native Association. Nunapitchuk had a rare and early educational opportunity. Through default there was a four-year period when the only teacher in the school was an Eskimo woman. This period of teaching paved the way for the following set of BIA teachers who also taught in terms of community education. One of these teachers married an Eskimo girl and at the time of this fieldwork had moved to Bethel where he was one of the leaders of the fishing co-op. The cooperative was given national news coverage when Walter Hickel, then governor of Alaska, under pressure from canneries in Seattle tried illegally to break it. When we consider the state school, we cannot ignore the very educating experience of this Eskimo cooperative.

ANCHORAGE, ALASKA'S BIG CITY

Anchorage is a boom town. It romantically likes to think of its boom as the derring-do of a latter day gold rush. Driving around Anchorage is more reminiscent of real estate developments around Seattle and the petty exploitation of millions of American dollars dumping inflation on the Arctic.

For the Eskimos, Anchorage is just a city, and they are in the minority as they would be in any city in the "Lower Forty-Eight." Five thousand Indians, Aleuts, and Eskimos live in Anchorage. Seven percent of the school population is Native. The superintendent of elementary education suggests that actual school attendance represents only a part of the Native population of school age. He claims that many children are not in school at all because Natives find the schools painful and unfriendly. This reflects clearly the fact that the public schools are not for Eskimos or other Natives. Education here is the most conventional White urban education, just as Anchorage city life is White urban society.

Overtones from our film suggest that we are looking at Native education in any middle-sized American city. Actually in Anchorage there is a lower percentage of non-White students than would be found in many American city schools today. There is a very small Black population in Anchorage and an even smaller Oriental community, so that Anchorage might be expected to be less sophisticated about educating ethnic minorities than many other American cities. Though Anchorage has the largest Native community in Alaska, this fact appears to have little or *no* effect on programming in the schools.

Possibly this is the educational tragedy of Alaska. Statistically the Eskimos are a very *small* group of people. They have as yet little political power. Only since the oil strike on the North Slope have their interests been an issue in Alaskan affairs. When viewing the Anchorage school film, it is hard to realize that this is Alaska. Even more than Bethel, Anchorage *is* the American experience. We can look at Natives in school here as affected by very much the same circumstances as in Oakland, Seattle, or Spokane. The simple fact is that Anchorage *really* is an American city. Its schools present a fair picture of Natives in school attendance anywhere in the country.

5 / The classrooms on film

The films themselves hold the drama of the Eskimo classroom. Methodologically we had distilled our impressions directly from film, analyzing frame for frame in many cases. What was on film was thus transferred to two hundred data sheets and coded statistically on key sort cards. But in the summary report that follows, describing the style and circumstances of each Eskimo classroom, film again becomes vitality and frees me to write both factually and empirically, drawing together in one picture many months of analysis.

TULUKSAK, AN ISOLATED BIA SCHOOL

Tuluksak was the smallest and most remote Eskimo village in our study. It had been selected because informants in the Chemawa Boarding School in Oregon said it had more of the survival economies than any other Kuskokwim village. I found upon arrival that there was *no* winter trapping going on, except by the VISTA worker's Eskimo assistant. Most of the village was on some variety of relief (which can be jeopardized by other sources of income) and during my winter visit there was literally no activity.

The BIA school was a compound of two classrooms, cafeteria, adjoining multi-purpose room, dispensary, radio room, guest room, and quarters for the teachers, whom we will call Mr. and Mrs. Pilot,[1] since the husband is an accomplished flyer. This couple had been teaching in Alaska twenty years and so might be considered representative of the BIA school culture.

Lower Grades

Mrs. Pilot was in command of a neat, well-equipped, and efficient classroom of about twenty students. The style of teaching was structured and very verbal. The teacher spoke distinctly in a well-modulated voice and kept the class going at a regimented pace. From a conservative point of view, this was a very well-taught class that should inspire a budding student teacher and delight educational superi-

---

[1] Descriptive code names have been devised to help the reader recall the many different characters in our drama.

April and May are bleak Arctic months on the Kuskokwim, but much schoolroom decoration follows the seasons of the South. Springtime in the "Lower Forty-Eight" is the motif for this bulletin board in the Tuluksak BIA school (right).

ors. Indeed, Mrs. Pilot's teaching was spoken of with admiration up and down the river and in faraway Chemawa.

In response to this verbal performance the students were very quiet, though fidgety with what might be boredom or withdrawal. They were well trained in their classroom roles, but looked a bit sleepy and as students, would be called dull. The team judgment describes the class as overstructured and overtrained in proper behavior, simply because there seemed no variation of behavior and very little spontaneous feedback from the students *to the teacher* or to one another.

One variation in the class routine was filmed. Once a week an old man from the village would come and tell stories in Eskimo. On this particular occasion the teacher set up the recorder to tape the story and then for a period left the room. Child-to-child communication changed. While they were intently listening to the Eskimo storyteller, the children formed a warm communicating group, expressing their acceptance of each other by body contact, hair caressing, and hand clasping.

Later the teacher brought in two Eskimo-made models of forest hunting camps, complete with canoe, meat cache, and forest tools. The children were immeditately involved in the models. But when the teacher took a pointer and began to ask questions, they reverted to classroom routine and waited and watched the lecturing-questioning of the teacher. Apparently the questioning distracted them from the model rather than stimulating them to look into the model. For a few moments the teacher's aide questioned the students, and they looked vividly at the model with considerable group communication.

During my visit this Eskimo teacher's aide usually remained very quiet, standing back or simply handing material to the class. I am sure she was much appreciated by Mrs. Pilot, but Mrs. Pilot's own style of teaching was so set that there was only limited work of a serious kind for her aide to do. Occasionally the Eskimo aide did take students into the cafeteria for special instruction. But considering Mrs. Pilot's teaching load in this two-room multigrade school, where there certainly was need for a real teaching assistant, why weren't these women teaching together? Because the aide didn't have a credential? Or was there simply no academic place for a Native teacher in the BIA school? These questions will be probed more deeply in our conclusions.

Mrs. Pilot went to great effort to have a colorful, freshly decorated room in keeping with the seasons. There were spring motifs (even in deep Arctic winter in the month of March) and child-play images: a choo-choo train hauling a long load of alphabets, a cutout line of circus figures, a calf drinking from a bucket of milk, a board with a huge bumblebee, and cutouts on a pinup board of the proper diet—Spanish rice, bread, butter, milk, and gingerbread, actually the menu for the school lunch. These were gay images of childhood, but they were not for Arctic children nor Arctic environment. One of Mrs. Pilot's survival lessons is not how to keep from getting lost in a blizzard but how to obey green and red stop-lights in Anchorage, taught with a full-size, green-yellow-red stop sign. The White school is dedicated to bringing modern knowledge to Eskimos. Mrs. Pilot was teaching White survival. Probably the only inadequacy of this "survival in Anchorage" lesson was the absence of a balancing lesson on survival within the Native world—an area probably outside Mrs. Pilot's cultural insights.

Visually the shortcoming in this room was that there was generally only teacher-to-student communication. There was no sense of a circuit interrelating everyone. Instead, the teacher was the center. She moved about constantly, send-

Culturally relevant learning of English stimulated by a model of an Eskimo camp in the BIA school in Tuluksak.

ing messages to individual students. But the students were as if alone in the room, barely projecting to the teacher and communicating with each other covertly or not at all.

Even this able and punctilious teacher did not manage to turn on this classroom. Yet, of all the BIA teachers in our sample, Mrs. Pilot had the *most* interaction with her village and had genuine friendships with various Eskimo women. She was *ambitious* for her students to excel, while at the same time discouraged about Tuluksak and the future of her students. We can surmise that despite the fact that Mrs. Pilot was an outstanding teacher in her own style, this did not appear to support the Eskimos' style, and that the students became much too uncommunicative and at the same time unreceptive.

Some time later I had occasion to film free-play in the village, and there was spontaneity and spirited behavior. The low pace of the classroom was replaced with delight and intensity.

Upper Grades

Mr. Pilot directed *his* class with equally seasoned professionalism. He appeared to have reduced education to its rudiments and leaned heavily on workbooks, which is not unreasonable in a mixed-graded classroom. His manner was gentle, quiet, and limited in verbal messages. He moved about the room constantly, briefly answering questions and correcting faults. In a quiet way he exerted *his* discipline, and the classroom was as structured as the first-through-fourth. He was very relaxed and his students equally relaxed. The research team described this behavior as sleepy. The team feels the students and teacher are just going through the motions. Actually this quiet teacher may have been giving more than the film reveals in-terms of education.

The walls of the classroom *do* reflect Alaska. There was a poster with samples of *all* fur-bearing animals, pelts glued on with the proper names of the animals. Above the blackboard were cutouts of Alaskan animals and a fleet of snowmobiles. Mr. Pilot is a flyer, hunter, and gunsmith, and probably the older boys relate to him on these skills. At least this was *one* bridge, and the eighth-grade students seemed genuinely involved in their tasks.

But despite these shared interests, the teacher stands aloof. He rarely sits down with his students and usually is in a state of motion. Our data sheets record *little direct evidence of student-teacher relations,* and it was observed that the workbook lessons seemed to require very few responses.

Despite evident competence, here also was a chasm with but a slender bridge— hunting and a flyer's involvement with the ecology—with a sense of great air space between teacher and student. Communication signals were very limited. The students did not watch the teacher or signal eye responses to the teacher. They did relate in a nonverbal way to one another; as one observer noted, they "yawned in unison."

Why was there so little to show for the human warmth of this school? Mrs. Pilot's kitchen door was always open, and women were often stopping to chat or have coffee with her. She was always simple and cordial and warm. In the evenings she helped run a weekly bingo game for the interested mothers and regularly held advisory school board meetings. In one meeting she stressed that soon the BIA might give up its educational function and the village might be expected to run its own school through a school board. Yet in the same meeting she read a long letter from the superintendent of BIA education asking whether the community wanted Native teachers. She presented the question by assuring them that there were not enough accredited Native teachers, so that if they wanted Native teachers they would have an unaccredited school. Since the majority agreed they did not want an unaccredited school, this amounted to *not* asking for Native teachers.

Had there been a formal path through the jungle of bureaucracy to practical goals of ethnic and ecological survival education, certainly teachers like Mr. and Mrs. Pilot would teach toward such goals. We have described how Mrs. Pilot did bring an Eskimo storyteller into the classroom. She made him very welcome and taped his Eskimo tales, which showed her appreciation of Eskimo stories she could not even understand. With explicit sanction from above, maybe many bush teachers would begin reaching out to Native teachers on many levels of content and skill.

Hovering in the background of the dedicated efforts to these two career bush teachers is the couple's shared conviction that there is little future for tiny Tuluksak simply because dollars and affluence are sweeping Alaska and somehow this progress spells doom for Eskimo communities. In a silent way maybe Tuluksak Natives feel this also, and so together teachers and students do not have much future to work toward. If there *were* a realistic future, probably these two teachers would change spontaneously the style of their teaching.

The Tuluksak case was one of the most baffling of our Eskimo study because of the ineffectiveness of the human potential of this teaching team; Mr. and Mrs. Pilot deserved their reputation as outstanding teachers, but still the school appeared failing the community. What was critically needed may be genuinely beyond the present intent and resources of the BIA or any White-administered Eskimo school. Education for Native welfare—missing from this school as from so many others—is inextricably involved with the conflict between two cultures and life styles.

Tuluksak is a community, but is its BIA school a community school? Is the lethargy of the community related to the pace of the school; or is the school the effect of the community? If it *were* a community school, what could it do for an underdeveloped community?

The community force in Tuluksak now is the Moravian lay minister, an Eskimo from the Kuskokwim Bay region on the Bering Sea. His efforts of community development are expressed in compulsive church attendance and study of the Bible. The BIA school appears in conflict with this church leader, and he has been reported to discourage community actions by the school. Hence the school on one very important level is isolated from the community. In a similar way the VISTA worker also ran into conflict with the church and found that *his* community program was quietly ignored by the village—to a point where the VISTA worker just sat alone in his cabin. As already stated, this is not always the case with BIA village schools; occasionally they *have* added to the community welfare in positive ways—though likely by circumnavigating BIA isolationism.

I revisited Tuluksak on May 3, just on the eve of the river breakup, indeed on the very last ski plane. The world was pools of melting snow, and great cakes of ice were beginning to move toward the sea. The silent winter village had sprung to life as more and more navigable water opened up along the village shore. Everywhere boats were being caulked, outboard motors repaired, nets mended, a canoe re-covered. Muskrat season was about to begin. Salmon fishing was weeks away. Everywhere children ran, danced, played marbles with young and old, played baseball, hovered around the water edge watching winter go out. Boats were finally launched in the limited clear water and motors began roaring as Eskimos raced up and down "to shake loose the ice." At this season it was hard to believe Tuluksak was doomed or had a low ebb of vitality at all. There was fire in Eskimo cheeks and sparkle in their eyes. How could there be a dull school in the midst of such vitality?

KWETHLUK, A PROGRESSIVE VILLAGE

"Kwethluk is different from Tuluksak. They're very progressive down there and busy. I think they have had some fine teachers there," observed Mrs. Pilot in Tuluksak. Kwethluk is fifteen air-minutes from Bethel. It is a large village with much involvement with the outside world and a number of career Eskimos working at status jobs in Bethel. In a sense Kwethluk is success-oriented and a village of cooperation.

Head Start: OEO (Funded by the Office of Economic Opportunity)

Our first filming was of the Head Start school, housed in a ramshackle planked building of spacious dimensions. This was the council house of Kwethluk and large enough to seat the adult population. The very setting made Head Start a village-dominated enterprise, in which there was much expressed community pride. As a model it was a "Village Community School," serviced by the community and taught by two young Eskimo women *of* the community. Except for a short summer workshop in Fairbanks, the teachers' education was the same as that of many adults who had also gone through the BIA high school programs at Mt. Edgecombe, Alaska or Chemawa, Oregon. Realistically it was a Native school taught by Native teachers and a very valuable opportunity for observing the educational potential of community education.

The first visual impression of the school interior was of its drabness and very limited equipment. An oil barrel converted into a wood stove gave meager heat. Long benches and a bare table were the only furniture. On one end was a walled closet area holding supplies. Though the day was overcast, blinding light reflected off the March snow pack, and the room was brilliantly lit.

Wearing stretch pants, the two teachers, Miss Annie Eskimo and Miss Betty Eskimo, were warming themselves around the stove when a father brought in his well-wrapped children for their day at school. Parkas were removed and soon the children were stomping off the snow in the anteroom and running eagerly to join a group seated on boxes around the teacher.

Watching the film silently without its accompanying tape, one would assume that the teacher was pursuing a very culturally determined curriculum, so shared and intense is the listening. Actually the curriculum was the standard Mother Goose! And the mime gestures given in unison were, we assume, standard kindergarten

OEO Head Start class in the village of Kwethluk, learning English from a book about Eskimo children.

material taught in any White school in America. Indeed we filmed other Mother Goose classes in BIA and state schools, but they were strikingly different in performance.

Here we observed the most fluent nonverbal communication filmed anywhere in our study. From teacher to student, from student *back* to teacher, and between student and student, the class was synchronized and wired together on one communication circuit so visible one could *see* a communication flow passing through this unified educational group.

First, there was body communication. Everyone was touching everyone else. Time lapse studies reveal synchronization of movement—leaning forward, leaning backward, holding forth a hand, rocking, swaying as one being, intense eye-to-eye communication, messaging by hand, touching, increasing communication by rearranging space.

For the children this was *home*, not a school. And later in free-play, clowning in adult clothing, stalking about in adult high pumps, children moved easily and fearlessly. *But discipline was in evidence,* signaled by a hand projected almost wordlessly, so that the morning passed in a sense of order and purpose.

There were ill children and some upset children who were tendered positive body affection and led to tasks by the hand, sat down at tables with a caress. But in spirit children were not *led* but motivated to move on their own momentum. A sick child was motivated to join the art session. Miss Annie Eskimo demonstrated

76

First grade in the BIA school in the village of Kwethluk.

the various colors possible with crayons, and then let the free-style drawing of the child's peers lead the timid student in graphic expression. Art work on the walls was all free style—collages, cutouts, and finger paintings. Here was the *only* art session filmed in Alaska where children were *not* coloring prepared Mother Goose dittoes.

Our team all rated this class as outstanding. We surmise that three circumstances were involved in this school's success. One, it was by default underequipped, which drew out special initiative from both teachers and students. Two, direction from above was very meager but empathetic. Ida Nicori, field representative of the regional Head Start office in Bethel, was a Kwethluk girl, so that the relationship all around was one of trust. The Head Start teachers were free to convert the experience into their own language and on their own terms. Three, the two teachers, with modest training, did not feel themselves *above* the village; rather they felt *part of* the village, which changed the conventional relationship between teacher, students, and parents.

I am sure they fulfilled most of the ideal expectations of child educators and the ideal of higher education courses in child development, but they did this in response to human function, not to theory. Their confident position spontaneously converted a hackneyed and often deadly Mother Goose routine into an Eskimo storytelling episode. The cultural self-determination *sensed* nonverbally was a determination of *style, pace,* and *rhythm* of the Eskimo way, which might make any curriculum palatable to Native children.

Prefirst in the BIA School

Two hundred yards from the village Head Start, Mr. Principal, principal of the BIA school, was instructing a prefirst class, also using the curriculum of Mother Goose. But the setting is radically changed. Mr. Principal is teaching this class in the absence of his wife, who is away on a medical leave.

Nowhere in America will you find a more modern, well-lit, and well-equipped school than the BIA plant in Kwethluk. It is technologically perfect, and painted in relaxing pastel shades. But Mr. Principal's large classroom is also shared by the second grade to accommodate another loss in teaching personnel.[2] At one end, second-graders lean over their workbooks, watched by the Eskimo teacher's aide, who stands quietly above the busy students, occasionally leaning down to help. At the other end, Mr. Principal is projecting Mother Goose images with an overhead projector to a sprawling class of prefirst students who are sitting on three lines of low chairs. Reading from a paper, he firmly singsongs the Mother Goose rhymes with his students, some in rhythm, some not, some looking about the room, gazing at the big enlargement of Little Bo Peep who lost her sheep. All-persuasive Mr. Principal tries to turn on his kids, while they *try* to sit still and concentrate on Little Bo Peep; indeed everyone seems *trying* together.

The film record shows very fractured communication. The teacher is earnestly and clearly projecting the message, but the words barely seem to make it over the chasm to the Eskimos. Reception signals are low. Eye reception is equally low. Faces were focusing in all directions, a few on the enlargement, a few on the teacher. Body behavior was equally distracted—feet flying out in all directions, some students slumped, some sitting straight, bodies twisting, leaning back, leaning forward. Mr. Principal's efforts seemed in vain. Each child was a distracted, unreceptive, uncommunicative individual, until a National Guard plane zoomed down on the nearby flying field—then senses synchronized and for a moment half the class was an intercommunicating group.

We are here observing the same curriculum but with a major difference. One, the teacher is a White man and a stranger, who has only been in the school less than a year. He has had very little contact with the villagers except in his classroom. Two, the teacher was standing while the students were seated in *rows.* Spacially, intercontact was all but impossible. The row seating disoriented the intergroup communication that might have been there if the children were sitting on the floor in a circle, with Mr. Principal as one element of this human circle. The result of this disorientation made each child a dislocated unit, and limp because he was not in a current flow of the group. Reception, concentration, and body control rapidly ran out and were replaced with dulling preoccupation and boredom. What if the Eskimo aide were to singsong alone with these kids? Would the circumstance have changed?

---

[2] The BIA school at Kwethluk was filmed on two field trips. On both occasions classes were very disturbed by the loss of two teachers and the consequent efforts to combine classes. Hence our records overlap the grade levels, but with different combinations on the two visits.

Teaching English by acting out Mother Goose rhymes in the OEO Head Start class in Kwethluk. Film clip illustrates body proximity and sensual unity of children learning together in a circumstance typical of a small-room culture, where living is usually within body reach in the small dwelling of the Arctic.

Head Start student in the village-run OEO school in Kwethluk. Home and school are a step apart; learning here begins at the door of the home.

The next session was an English language class based on a supposedly practical situation.[3] Written on the blackboard in large letters:

Good morning Mr. Policeman.
My name is ——————.
Good morning. Can I help you?
Can you direct me to the Hospital?
Yes, I can.
Thank you.

[3] I have been told since that the policeman lesson was drawn from a TESL (Teaching English as a Second Language) program prepared for Spanish-speaking Puerto Rican children in New York City; as such it makes more sense, both in regard to situation and linguistics, since the rather stilted "direct me" makes use of the Spanish cognate *"dirigirme."*

Is this a situation an Eskimo child might meet in the streets of Anchorage? Mrs. Pilot in Tuluksak had an illuminated stop-and-go sign to alert children to survival in cities; Mr. Principal had a standard educational tool—a cardboard image of a policeman with a hole for the face to frame the head of the Eskimo child, so *each* child could be Mr. Policeman. A martyr was drawn from the group, his head thrust through the cardboard policeman image. Looking sheepish, the martyr and another recruit repeated, reading from the board, "Good morning, Mr. Policeman. My name is John." And so on through the sequence. Then still another child was drawn from the group to say to the cardboard "Good morning, Mr. Policeman."

Again Mr. Principal used the greatest persuasion—physically standing the children face to face. Turning to the group, he enunciated very distinctly and corrected their responses with gestures of encouragement and criticism. Psychologically, when these gestures are looked at frame for frame, they turn out not to be gestures to draw communication together; rather they seemed to be pushing the children even further away.

We evaluate this class knowing there was great stress in this school. Two teachers had left. It was near the end of a long winter. Mr. Principal was, no doubt, worried about his wife. I was warned the school would be tense, and realistically I had filmed this tension projected into the classroom, tension that was no doubt widening further the gap already lying between school and community. We cannot dismiss this as an unusual circumstance, however, for all too frequently there is stress in the compounds. This stress should be expected, realistically, as one of the barriers that arise between isolated White teachers and the Arctic community.

Despite the internal strife, the BIA school in Kwethluk held up remarkably in dedication and educational skill. The stress of the principal substituting for his ill wife does not negate the effort that he put into trying to make his school a success. The performance of other Kwethluk teachers speaks for the goals of his administration.

Lower Grades: BIA

The first three grades and the eighth grade were taught by Mrs. and Mr. Kweth. Both received a high ranking by the research team. I believe they were equally isolated from the village but were well-oriented and disciplined teachers. Maybe *too* disciplined, but they did not break under the circumstance and kept their classes on a high level; overdiscipline may have been a survival essential.

First grade was taught along with second and third. This demands programming. The classes were scattered about the room in groups, some with workbooks, some with earphones listening to audio lessons. First grade was gathered around a table with the teacher. As one researcher noted, "She camouflaged herself by sitting low with her students." The class was relaxed and not teacher dominated. Communications from the teacher were directed verbally to individuals or to small groups, so that the room remained open for relaxed student-to-student communication. Students felt free to get up, look out the window, talk to one another in a reasonable way. Researchers agreed it was a happy class and an open class.

Upper Grades: BIA

Across the hall Mr. Kweth taught eighth grade. In many ways this was an invaluable filming opportunity. When I set up my camera, it appeared I would be recording a very rigid situation—a multigrade class of sixth, seventh, and eighth grade students sitting compactly behind desks. Mr. Kweth took a teaching position at the head of this large class group, and because of the way the seating was arranged, there seemed little opportunity but to lecture. And that was what Mr. Kweth proceeded to do, never once leaving his position or asking or accepting any response from the students. Might this be just the approach to turn off bewildered Eskimo students? But Mr. Kweth was not only a good lecturer; he had chosen what turned out to be a swinging subject—*mental health*—with a heavy accent on the deprivations of life in the "Lower Forty-Eight."

On film can be seen the effect of *relevance*. As one researcher noted, "Mental health is ego-oriented." This must be true, for here was the longest concentration span of *any* class in our sample. Despite a fairly dry delivery, the class rarely took their eyes from the teacher except to make notes. The level of intellectual intensity cannot be matched by any high school class I filmed in Bethel or Anchorage. The teacher proceeded to diagram the health of Kwethluk village, showed the whole world related to Kwethluk, and stressed the importance of *family*, village *cooperation*, and positive human relationships.

Apparently this found sophisticated ears and may have touched the mainsprings of village vitality. Communication within the group was intense. Reception was visually clear from ear to eye to notebook, and there was free intergroup communication. Notes were compared, books were shared (a social studies text around which the lecture was composed), and the student-to-student communication was *about* the lesson, either sharing notes or audio and body communications while eyes were clearly focused on the teacher.

In Kwethluk there were two amazing extremes: first, communication and empathy converting ·an irrelevant curriculum into an exciting experience in Head Start, and second, a highly motivating and relevant curriculum turning on Eskimo students despite a dull and exhausting teaching method—the lecture. I do not suppose Mr. Kweth has this good circumstance of relevance every day, but this day was the positive record of what can take place when Eskimo children relate to the message.

Middle Grades: BIA

Later I filmed fourth and fifth grades taught by Mr. Luk, and by combining relatedness, clear two-way communication, *and* relevance, Mr. Luk had one of the happiest classes in the BIA sample. Only one White teacher in the regular classes rated higher in terms of communication.

What was involved in Mr. Luk's class? First in importance was a great diversity in communication, on the part of the teacher and in return, on the part of the students. Mr. Luk used clear verbal communication, explicit nonverbal hand, body, and arm signaling, and he constantly changed, adjusting himself in space to improve and complete communication. He would move from the front of the class directly to a respondent, lean over and speak personally with this student. Other times he directed himself to small groups. Then he would communicate with the class at large. Students freely approached him, drew him to their problems, or helped themselves to materials when they needed them. Mr. Luk switched from verbal to visual techniques rapidly—pointing to the clock or moving hands on a demonstration clock, drawing a foot on the board and relating it to the student's foot.

Students worked intensely, writing, reading, computing, working at the chalkboard with visible enthusiasm. This high spirit was expressed in communicating with each other, by body relating, eye signaling, and work sharing. When tension got too high for some students, they clowned and fooled around, yet were not pounced on by the teacher. In body motion there were no signals of boredom or sleepiness and many body signals projected work involvement, such as body bending intently over work or moving to improve reception from the teacher.

There was a fire drill. The school poured out into the yard. And then an all-clear. The whole class ran spiritedly back to the classroom as if eager to continue their projects.

Around tne walls were large art drawings, made by the students, of the history of ancient civilizations, including the Aztecs and Mayas. One felt Mr. Luk had a

Dedicated, well-trained teachers put great effort into their task. A sixth grade teacher in a BIA village school.

lively imagination and driving educational interests that were projected to the students.

Tuluksak and Kwethluk BIA Schools Compared

There is a temptation to compare the Tuluksak with the Kwethluk BIA school. The comparison is not easy to make in terms of educational skill and dedication. All the teachers at Kwethluk were in their first year of teaching in the Arctic They were from a different generation—knew *more* on one hand and *much less* on another in terms of the long-range development of Native potential in the Arctic. Educationally this worked in favor of the Kwethluk school, for lack of self-fulfilling knowledge about Eskimos allowed them to work ideally and put out units of energy that would be unrealistic for old Alaska hands. Mr. and Mrs. Pilot had been twenty years watching the ebb and flow of the BIA. If they were not cynical, they certainly were philosophical about the realistic limitations of village schooling. They each had a rich fund of historical knowledge and years of living with the benign failure of the BIA. Their very insight into history and the Eskimos seemed to temper their efforts and had the effect of quietly limiting the scope of their teaching to what they perceived as reality.

The Kwethluk staff have scattered now. Two, I believe, are still in the Arctic. But the Pilots are still in Tuluksak, no more disillusioned than they were in the spring of 1969, giving the same warmth and day-by-day generosities to their village.

The Moravian Children's Home, Near Kwethluk

The Moravian Home and School is just three miles from busy Kwethluk, but years away in time and culture. There is little to compare between the BIA school and this mission project. Issues of change hardly stir the Home, other than shifting from dog team to gasoline snowmobile to fetch the mail in winter. I cannot imagine that any change has come to its classrooms for the last twenty years. One of the teachers is the daughter of an early Moravian missionary couple who raised their family on the Kuskokwim. She teaches fifth through eighth grades. Kwethluk Eskimos speak with respect of this school—tough training, high standards, no games.

The research team had only negative comments on the first- to fourth-grade class. The school is, of course, frugal and poorly equipped, but this did not explain the totally drab, brown-on-brown interior of this small classroom, where very young children come to learn. The teacher was friendly but inept, and seemed unable to reach her young students. They sat dutifully, some yawning, all trained to look occupied, though none of the research team felt they were. The film clearly showed that they were simply acting busy. They sat reasonably still, but their eyes were not focused on books or on the speaking teacher. Their focus was dead, nondirective, and sleepy. There was a lot of fidgeting, but always within a safe level so that they still *appeared* to be attending the lesson.

The teacher was tethered to her desk and made only short forays out, snapping back as if on a rubber band, as if this tiny class were threatening. One data sheet reads, "Maybe just letting time pass." Professionally she appeared as just an unmotivated and poorly trained, or possibly untrained, White, middle-class teacher. Communication was superverbal with almost no other expressions by arm, body, smile, or eye contact.

Only one student seemed absorbed; he was leafing through a book about Eskimos. The class text was the usual dreary White boy-and-girl story, and there was simply nothing in the room to remind the viewer that this school was completely surrounded by the white Arctic winter.

The second class, fifth through eighth, was held in a large but desk-crowded room. The effect of the room was more brown-on-brown, with an American flag, a piano, a few religious pictures, and odd decorations like cutout bunnies that in no way related to each other. The room, like the rest of the Home, was anti-aesthetic but clean, well-scrubbed, varnished and waxed. Twenty-five students, boys and girls, worked at their desks. A few showed signs of stress, as one might expect in a home for displaced children. Many more were relaxed and looked genuinely happy.

The research team felt that this missionary teacher and her students were closer together than most students and teachers in the BIA schools. They felt the teacher was quite secure with her students and that the room had a relaxed trusting air. The teacher communicated verbally, with only a few nonverbal arm signals, and freely drew upon students to act out lessons for the class. Students were receptive to the teacher, and thus one form of education was happening in this school. There was communication in this room, even though it was basically one way. Students *did* get her messages, listening was real, attention spans were reasonably long. Unquestionably much education *could* take place in this room. In fact the Moravian Home as an institution has this rich potential. If it fails, then the fault is purely philosophical.

"Provincial" would describe the style of the Moravian Home, and the relating was definitely family oriented, as if everyone genuinely depended on one another. The quality of education sprang from this and set the character of the school apart from the BIA, where the teachers only needed the students to teach and the students needed the school only so long as they sat there. Here there was no gulf between school and community because the community *was* the school.

THE ALASKA STATE SCHOOL IN BETHEL

This consolidated elementary and high school is housed under one roof and directed by one superintendent. Although there is a principal of elementary education and a principal of the high school, the joint effect on Eskimo education is genuinely that of *one* school.

Eighty-five percent of the student body *is* Eskimo, so in one sense it *is* an Eskimo extended community school. The other 15 percent, the White students, are largely marginal and migratory. Many are from temporary families involved in Fish and Game, Civil Aeronautics, Public Health, and the BIA. The few more stationary White families with schoolchildren are schoolteachers, ministers, town officials, and storekeepers. The presence of the White students offers us the opportunity to observe White-Eskimo relationships in education and suggests patterns of school integration where Eskimos can interact educationally with White students. It also reveals how teachers respond to *both* Eskimos and White students. Is there a pre-ferential relationship? Does the small White minority in the student body make this state school appreciably different from a smaller model of a BIA Eskimo com-munity school?

The Community as School

Eskimos are in Bethel for a range of reasons. First, Bethel must be viewed as an acculturation way-point *out* of Eskimo village culture into the world beyond. Second, Bethel symbolizes Eskimos' efforts to meet modern economic change in the Arctic and to organize themselves in new associations capable of extending Eskimo solidarity into the economic future. Bethel is the site of the effectual Kuskokwim fishing cooperative. A construction company that builds model homes for Eskimos on the assembly line also has been training Natives in the construction trades under the Manpower Development Training Act.

Eskimos also come to Bethel to pursue education. Traditionally, Bethel has been the educational center for religious training by the Moravian Church. Now families move in from isolated villages so that their children can go through high school without leaving for distant BIA boarding schools.

Bethel has a large, permanent, urban Eskimo population involved in various job occupations and in some businesses. Eskimos work for the city, the BIA, the Na-tional Guard, Public Health, OEO, Fish and Game, Alaska Rural Development and VISTA programs, the municipal airport, and in all the various stores and commercial undertakings. One Eskimo family has a Standard Oil sales contract. Finally, Bethel has a blossoming relief community with an authentic Eskimo slum.

But Bethel *is* an Eskimo community variously affected by Eskimo life styles. Eskimo home clusters have the typical Eskimo bathhouses. A community hall regularly has Eskimo gatherings with Eskimo food and Eskimo drumming, singing, dancing, and mime acting entertainment. There is a large active Eskimo Dog Sled Racing Association, and aggressive membership in the Alaskan Native Association. Eskimo groups also carry out traditional salmon fishing through the summer months. Both the Cooperative and representatives of Seattle canneries buy tons of salmon every season.

The School as the Focal Point of Education

All this community environment in one way or another affects the total educa-tion of Bethel's Eskimo children. But to what extent do all these heterogeneous community activities *affect* the school and in particular the teachers in the school?

Education as formal schooling was not much affected by Eskimo Bethel, for in so many ways the teachers were as isolated from the community as they were in the villages. Despite the fact that Bethel is a key hub of air transportation in the Arctic, with jet planes roaring in and out all day long; despite the fact that Bethel is an essential defense hub with a large armory that administers a multi-tude of National Guard centers; and despite the fact that outwardly Bethel is an Eskimo community as were the villages, Bethel is actually a White town administered essentially by and for White people. It is not an integrated community. Far from it. Bethel is broken down into not just *one* White compound that could be compared with the traditional BIA school compound, but *five* equally segregated White compounds, each essentially separate from the town of Bethel socially and geographically. The Public Health Hospital has its wholly separate, self-contained compound, an ex-radar site, four miles from town. The Fish and Game Commission and Civil Aeronautics Board *each* have their compounds three miles out on the tundra. And the school has *its* trailer-teacher compound behind the school a mile from the town's commercial center. This means *all* these White therapeutic, educational, and bureaucratic operations have their walls of isolation from the Eskimo community that can be compared to those of the BIA village school.

Compound culture was constantly reinforced by the growing White specialist population and the nearly complete lack of housing in the town of Bethel. Here conditions spoke of the Alaska frontier with makeshift, unhygienic housing totally inappropriate to the needs of imported teachers, doctors, specialists, and administrators. So, in a sense, there *had* to be compounds, just as there *had* to be compounds in the villages, creating the same self-fulfilling isolation of teachers, nurses, and doctors as was observed in the BIA village schools.

Quite symbolically, one major reason *not* to live in Bethel proper, even when possible, was the town's liquor store, which was essential to the economic well-being of the town through its contribution to taxes and equally essential to the White people in the compounds who needed both the tranquilization and the escape of alcohol. But at the same time "living downtown" was both unpleasant and "dangerous" because "there are so many drunk Eskimos. . . . Natives just don't know how to handle liquor!"

Probably the most effectual school in Bethel was the Public Health Maternity Center that *was* located in the midst of Eskimo Bethel. Eskimo women would stay in this clinic for a few weeks *before*, as well as after, their babies were born. The home and clinic was a therapeutic-educational community directed by a PH nurse who *did* associate wholly, professionally, and humanly with Eskimos in this center.

The Bethel school, on the other hand, through numerous intents and defaults, was on the *edge* of the community. Eskimo children, as in the villages, left their shacks by the river and walked into a wholly contrasting life style designed to educate them for a successful future. *But this future was White not Eskimo.* There italics are not a value judgment that Eskimo life style is the only right style for Eskimos, but simply to define an alienation-communication problem that can beset the Eskimo child in this well-run and best-taught White school.

We will report on the school as one effort, singling out only special classes that seem to set the dimensions of the culture.

Kindergarten

Film entry into the school was through the kindergarten. Here a career Alaska teacher past middle age directed a class of some twenty Eskimo and part-Eskimo children. Mrs. Kinderbelle was eager that I visit her class: "This is the day an Eskimo always comes and plays for our class so the children can dance." I opened the door to loud electronic music and found an unsmiling Eskimo playing an electric guitar in front of a group of seated children. The children were separated by sexes, boys in the front row, girls in the back row; throughout the kindergarten filming, boys and girls continued to be separated whether sitting in rows or at tables. This was in contrast to both Head Start and prefirst in Kwethluk. One embarrassed boy was standing and supposedly dancing. To implement this, the teacher took him forcibly by the shoulders and propelled him through a series of steps, while she—still grasping the boy—stomped and pirouetted to the music. Letting go, the teacher sat down with a little smile while the boy dragged his feet around the floor. His chore over, he quickly returned to Mrs. Kinderbelle and received a chocolate that was the reward for dancing. Now two small girls were pushed into the room and, sucking fingers sheepishly, shuffled their feet. They, in turn, received the rewarding chocolates. This routine continued while the class sprawled in their seats, pretty much ignoring what was going on. The amplified music continued ceaselessly without any communication between the Eskimo musician, the children, or the teacher.

This routine was broken by recess time. Parkas were grabbed. Boys lined up on one side, girls in another line, ready to leave the room. At this point Mrs. Kinderbelle busied herself in a closet so that her back was turned. Suddenly several girls joined hands and began dancing. On film one can see that *their whole bodies are involved,* from light springing steps to rocking bodies to faces transfixed with delight. As suddenly as the teacher turned, saw the activity, and raised a finger, the dancing stopped, and the kids were back in line. Now the teacher took a position in front of the boys' line and opened the gate for the girls to go out first. As if with freedom in sight, the girls literally bounded out of the door dancing and gesturing with delight. This behavior was not picked up by the boys, who shuffled out of the room without expression.

The class returned to a midmorning milk break and as if refreshed by the winter cold of the play yard, sat down with enthusiasm to eat pilot crackers and drink reconstituted milk. Again boys and girls were in separate parts of the room. On the part of the girls this was a refreshing change from the earlier class behavior. They gathered round their tables in congenial groups with much communication bodily and verbally, which seems spontaneous for Eskimo children. There were hugs and whispered messages. Then in a melodic unit one table of girls toasted each other with milk, touching glasses again and again, transformed into an intimate coordinating group reminiscent of Head Start in Kwethluk.

The boys in this class seemed more oppressed than the girls, but for both groups it was vividly clear that these children were turned off and even humiliated by Mrs. Kinderbelle. They were resisting communication between each other whenever the teacher exerted her leadership.

Kindergarten Music

Later the music teacher, director of the Bethel High School band, made his weekly visit to kindergarten to teach singing. Mr. Music was a tall, lanky man who literally towered over the little Eskimos seated on low stools, again in two rows. Mr. Music was a new teacher from the "Lower Forty-Eight," charged with zeal and enthusiasm. "Old MacDonald had a farm. E-I, E-I, O," was the theme today. With grimacing face and clowning hands the teacher acted out the words while singing the tune in a high nasal voice. The girls giggled and wagged their hands in response and a few actually carried the tune. The boys were less responsive, yawned, careened around in their chairs, while one boy made clowning grimaces himself, directed at the camera. When this boy wandered from his seat, Mr. Music pounced down from above and placed him solidly where he belonged and continued his "E-I, E-I, O" routine. The students looked amused but on the whole just mystified.

Next came the alphabet song. Children in turn stood by an alphabet board, and while the group sang the familiar melody, which they seemed to have memorized, they pointed to the "A, B, C, D, E, F, G. . . ." But there is a catch in this rhyme. When the child came to "Q, R, S, and . . ." he would point to the "T." They knew the melody and the counting process, but they did not yet relate the names of the letters to the actual letters, nor did they realize that "and" was not a letter name. Each time the teacher forcibly pointed the child's finger at the *right* letter, the melody would break, the rhythm would be lost, and the child would complete the cycle in a perfunctory, crestfallen manner.

In this class we were constantly seeing teachers pouncing on the free-style behavior of children, shattering group solidarity and communication. Children were forced into isolated units of one, where they are both embarrassed and thwarted. Children were being *forced* to do this, forced to do that, and each time they would slump. We cannot forget the Head Start class with its rhythmic nursery rhymes with teacher and students acting out meanings together. Mr. Music was a very warm, well-meaning and dedicated teacher. He *liked* his job and renewed his contract, but he was unable to set up free two-way communication in this kindergarten. For one thing there was no way for Mr. Music to understand the style of Eskimo childhood and play rhymes, and he approached this class as if oblivious that his students were Eskimo.

Two First Grades

Two classes were filmed, and the contrasting background and performance of the two teachers may hold clues as to the character of teaching that Eskimo children respond to.

One first-grade teacher, Mrs. Bethel, was the wife of the school superintendent. She and her husband are very active in the Moravian Church and live in what used to be the Moravian Mission compound. Mrs. Bethel could be compared with Mrs. Pilot at Tuluksak, for both women approached their classroom with similar professionality, a scheme of teaching that begets orderly behavior, a high level of teacher direction, and a programmed procedure that is perfectible and predictable.

Communication in Mrs. Bethel's class was freer than in the Tuluksak first grade but equally *verbal*. Mrs. Bethel did accomplish discipline. Students remained in their seats, and the teacher circulated around to *them* rather than having the students come freely to *her*. Much of her class was storytelling by phonograph record and illustrated from a picture book that she held on high and made a great effort for everyone to *see*. She also *read* a story and created a more intimate group than the record sequence. The students remained quite *motionless* before her in this group, of which Mrs. Bethel was physically a part. The group *could* have communicated to each other by touch but did not, nor did Mrs. Bethel touch the children. There was little body motion, but head focus did suggest *listening*.

Later an experimental group came from the seventh grade and *played* teacher. The room was broken down into small groups around upper classmen who *directed* various number and word games with cards. One ambitious Eskimo girl drew her group closely around her and communicated intensely—verbally and by eye and body signaling. This student-teaching-student situation radically changed the learning structure. Not only were small groups formed, but they tended to get *down on the floor* to sprawl in convenient perceptive and receptive positions. Space was radically adjusted for ideal communication. Both the student-teachers and the students communicated vividly and appeared excited by this unusual learning situation.

Mrs. Artist, the other first-grade teacher, was a long-time resident of Alaska and Bethel. Her husband had once been a BIA teacher but was now a state representative from Bethel with a vested interest in Eskimo welfare. The couple had four daughters who had made close friends with Eskimos and who danced Eskimo dances with their Native friends at community gatherings. Mrs. Artist also was interested in art and drew and painted, herself.

It was immediately evident that Mrs. Artist was concerned about communication in her classroom. Desks were all facing each other in rows, presumably to increase the interaction between students in her room. Instead of facing the teacher, they faced each other.

The first minutes of film are not exceptional. The class was relaxed, busy, and responsive to the teacher and each other. But as the film continues a number of exceptional elements appear. One, the teacher rarely stands *above* her students, but works at eye level, very much the way that Mrs. Kweth worked with her class in Kwethluk. Second, Mrs. Artist rarely teaches to the whole group but rather to *units* of the class, which puts education not on a one-to-many but rather a one-to-a-few and many times a one-to-one communicating relationship. Third, the class did a lot more individually involved study. This means *communication between the student and himself*. This was dramatized by the class recess, during which a lone Eskimo boy worked on with pencil and notebook, oblivious of the departure of the class.

In Mrs. Pilot's class in Tuluksak and in Mrs. Bethel's first grade here, children were *wholly absorbed with the teacher* or else daydreaming. In Mrs. Artist's class many students were wholly absorbed directly with the study at hand. And finally, body motion was free, as it was when the upper-grade students acted as teachers in Mrs. Bethel's class. Body movement was not directionless contortions and fidgeting; body posture was directly related to attention on study tasks or adjusting for better reception. Rodin's "Thinker" rests hand on chin—a thinking posture. Kids when turned on to tasks seek similar postures that affect circulation and intensity of concentration.

Mrs. Artist and her husband began teaching Eskimos in the villages, and she has retained this character of relationship in her classroom in Bethel.

Three Male Teachers: Two Fifth Grades and a Second Grade

As the proportion of Caucasian students to Eskimos increases, contrasting behavior became more evident. One second-grade and two fifth-grade classes compared also describe basic styles of education that succeed in turning Eskimo students on or turning them off. These three Bethel teachers presented similarities and contrasts that define one major teaching problem—how to relate to Native students. One of these fifth-grade teachers was on his first contract in Alaska, the other on his second, but neither appeared to have solved this challenge as yet. The second-grade teacher, on his third contract, *had* mastered this relating. He had taught in an Indian community in Southeast Alaska before coming to Bethel.

Mr. Foreman related to his fifth-grade class by assuming an aloof manner that justified distance and could be called "the shop foreman" approach. "Leave them on their own. They have their job to do and I have mine." But at the same time he expects his workers to turn out perfect parts to specification. Mr. Foreman's desk is *behind* his students in one rear corner, as if to say, "Don't bother me with your personal problems—just get on with the production." Do his worker-students mistrust him? There is an air of repression which inhibits students from communicating with one another or from peacefully settling down to their work, as if one ear were turned to the foreman and only part of their attention were on their work. Mr. Foreman feels he is a disciplined man who is treating his workers in a fair, realistic manner. Actually his position may have been one of great insecurity. He can watch the students but they cannot watch him without turning around, which makes his desk a spy vantage point.

Curriculum content during the filming was a barrage of questions fired at the backs of the students: "How is a whale like a man?"—in an effort to elicit the logic of biological typology. Students do not have workbooks in front of them or assigned jobs, so that the teacher's approach seemed defeating except in offering him a special role. Later, the material shifted to how words are put together—again, an open-ended, highly verbal approach without workbooks. Occasionally Mr. Foreman strolled out from his desk up and down the aisles, inspected the students' progress, but rarely paused, and always returned to the security of his desk in the back of the room.

The results were chaotic, with a great deal of fidgeting and a very low communication *back* to the teacher. Because Mr. Foreman was also a disciplinarian, there was no communication or collaboration *between* students and there was a sense of tension that did not inspire independent student-to-himself thinking. Furthermore, with the high incidence of deafness among Eskimo children and inasmuch as *all* hard-of-hearing spontaneously lip-read, this behind-the-back supervision must have been a double hardship for some.

This teaching routine avoids the problem of relating to the Eskimo student, and Mr. Foreman appeared very thwarted, for his position made recognizing and communicating personally with his class impossible.

Mr. Professor, the second fifth-grade teacher, faced his class *all* the time in a standing position at the front of the room. He used a lecture and leading question approach on the subject of the geography and history of the Western United States—the last spike on the transcontinental railroad, the use of irrigation in the Imperial Valley, and so on. Though a surprising number of students do answer questions, the data sheets describe a yawning, fidgety class, many always looking down, with signals of very short attention span. Toward the end of class a student got up and left in the middle of the teacher's question.

Mr. Professor's classroom manner could be compared with that of the eighth-grade teacher in Kwethluk, who also lectured without moving from the front of the room. But there was a difference. In Kwethluk, Mr. Kweth appeared genuinely aware that he was teaching Eskimos, conducted the lessons on their terms, and got a turned-on class. Mr. Professor did not seem aware his students were Eskimos. He was teaching competently about White America as if to White children to whom it was familiar; it is amazing he got the response that he did. The four White children in his geography class seemed reasonably attentive, but he seemed unaware that most of his Eskimo students were distracted, apathetic, and continually yawning Both these teachers were competent and dedicated. Both faced the same cultural barrier. Mr. Kweth, on his first Alaskan assignment, tried to cross it intellectually. Mr. Professor, who came to Alaska in 1960, appeared in this circumstance to ignore it. So we observe that despite years of teaching of Eskimo children, unless the culture chasm is recognized, it may never be effectually crossed.

What happens when a teacher crosses the frontier back into childhood? The film of Mr. Scout's second-grade class was a record of teacher and students sharing a world together. An Eskimo world? Or just childhood? In terms of early chilhood education it hardly matters. But, of course, the gulf between cultures *had* to be crossed, or the teacher could not have entered the children's world.

The sound tape opens with a every high noise volume of children's voices, and the film records a pandemonium of contrasting activities that marks the end of a class period. Mr. Scout is calmly walking through his students to get his parka from the clothes rack. He cups his hands so he can be heard above the din: "Boys and girls, leave everything the way it is, because I have to go out to recess with you!" Winter clothing is put on, fur ruffs pulled about faces, and most of the class follows him *out*. But various students stay behind, too involved with tasks under way to stop. Also, snacks must be readied; paper cups, napkins, and pilot biscuits, passed around. A busy team is at work, pouring milk, arranging food—very self-contained and self-directed.

A second period begins with students munching pilot biscuits at their desks. "Now I am going to read you a story while you eat." The story? *The Husband Who Was to Mind the House.* Mr. Scout settles himself comfortably in a chair at the head of the room to read, with appropriate gestures, this old classic of a husband's *trying* to do his wife's job, while the cow moos and the pig tips over the butter churn. Children munch and listen. Nothing very relevant here? Well, there was nothing particularly relevant in Old Mother Goose in the Kwethluk Head Start either.

In studying Mr. Scout's class we are observing substance on the further side of relevance. The space surrounding this teacher and his class is closed space that contains *both* teacher and students.

Apparently there was more order and planning than the observer could pick up readily. After the story the teacher directed students, "Now the violet group may work on their story or stories," and the class broke down in small units, violet, green, and so on. Each child knew what was expected of him.

There are also single students involved in their own tasks. A long roll of paper is rolled out on the floor and students continue writing and drawing. Mr. Scout moves from individual to individual, from group to group. He leans over, sits down, touches, corrects, and moves on. Students run to *him* with papers. He pauses, ponders, gives criticism, settles down by another group of students. Studying the tape it becomes obvious that many projects are under way at various levels. This room *feels* like an ungraded room with everyone working at his own speed.

The teacher appears very relaxed, speaks in a conversational tone, gets down to eye level, and talks slowly *to* students. There are no signs of boredom, no yawning. Everyone is *busy,* and the room appears like a well-oiled machine with multiple parts all moving continuously, but with different functions and speeds.

Examining this class as *communication,* we find every variant means of communicating taking place. The teacher projects vividly to the whole class, verbally and nonverbally, to units of the class, and to individuals. Student-to-teacher communicating takes place verbally and by physical contact as was observed in Head Start. The teacher clearly responds. He stops moving, leans down, touches sender, completes message, before he moves on. Students communicate together in study and creativity, sometimes in groups, sometimes one to one. And many students work alone, *communicating with themselves,* self-contained, oblivious of others.

How does this teacher relate? We observed him directing the Bethel Boy Scouts. Is *this* an empathetic, culturally determined activity—Boy Scouting? Mr. Scout went through the patriotic routines with dignity, but gently, and in talking scouting made no special concessions to his Eskimo troop for being Eskimo.

But looking deeper, we find that Mr. Scout *likes children,* and in turn likes *Indian* and *Eskimo* children. Their welfare consumes most of his professional and free time. Mr. Scout was eased out of his first job in the state school system in an Indian community reportedly *because he spent too much time with the Natives,* often spending the weekend living with Indian family friends. This is very different from collecting harpoons and Eskimo masks. Maybe Mr. Scout does not need to collect these trophies, the main value of which is that they *prove* that the owner has made it to Alaska.

White Students in Eskimo Classes

There was one seventh-grade general science class that was about half Eskimo and half White. This class is the most confusing in the study, with free projective behavior of students that suggest some concise patterns separating Eskimo boys from White boys and Eskimo girls from White girls.

This class was taught by an empathetic teacher who had served in the Peace Corps and was one of three Bethel teachers who lived down in the village. Mr. Mike's manner was permissive and relaxed, which added to the spontaneous groupings in this classroom.

The film opens with Mr. Mike preparing to carry out a chemical experiment, his desk at the front of the room but turned toward the right hand sector of the room away from the windows. Three Eskimo boys and one White boy sit on the far left by the windows, where it is literally impossible to watch the experiments at the teacher's desk. Two other White boys sit ten feet or more away across from the Eskimos on seats near the back of the room. Three White girls and an Eskimo girl sit in rows to the right of the boys, and four Eskimo girls sit together along the wall. There is a lot of shifting around by White boys, but this is the general pattern.

The Eskimos and one White boy appear to have taken seats freely, *outside* the class, where participation is difficult or impossible. Though the White boy near the window moves during the filming, the Eskimos remain by the window.

The four White boys goof off all through class, shift about, and generally show little interest in the experiment. One White girl shows interest and makes notes, but the other three White girls show no interest at all. One polishes her nails, and one openly reads a sexy paperback novel. *All* the Eskimo girls seem involved in the experiment, watch the teacher's lips, and make copious notes. The Eskimos by the window just sit, smile, and look out the window. The teacher ignores their presence and turns all his attention to the girls.

We feel the distraction in this room and the peculiar patterned behavior is related to the fifty-fifty Eskimo-White student body. The predominant Eskimo style fell off, and aggressive White male style began to intrude. This in turn affected the behavior of the White girls. The fifty-fifty division totally confused the programming of this class.

Special Education

Special Education for deaf and retarded children makes up a separate unit of the Bethel school. Here is a wholly different view of education that puts these Special Ed classes *outside* the conventions of White education for Native children.

There are no special opportunities for handicapped children in the villages, and the BIA boards Eskimo children in Bethel to take advantage of a rapidly growing program for handicapped children within the state consolidated school. There are four Special Ed classrooms and plans for immediate enlargement of the program, so great is the demand for such classes. Deafness is a major problem for Eskimo children because of an unexplained high incidence of punctured ear drums. Infections in babyhood are suspected of causing this handicap.

The research team unanimously rated Special Ed classes as the most effectual in the Bethel sample and felt they held significant approaches that could benefit education for all Eskimo children. This is not unrealistic. Attitudes essential in Special Education of the retarded and the deaf are by necessity directed to the welfare of the individual child. *His* emotional and intellectual welfare is the issue. Other conventional socioeconomic goals so emphasized in public education are of little importance to the disturbed or deaf child. His success as a human being *is* the achievement of educational development.

With this perspective, Eskimo children in Special Ed get the very attention they commonly fail to get in the regular classroom, where the compulsion to push the Native child *into* the economic system of the dominant society is so great that in the process the Eskimo child can be destroyed as a successful human being. The class for the deaf and the class for the retarded, each has a character of its own, but both classes seem designed to offer the maximum personality fulfillment of each student.

The Deaf Class Experience

The tape of the deaf class has few verbal communications between teacher and student, but the film shows fluent nonverbal relating that gives this class a rich sense of communication. Ironically there is more two-way communication in this handicapped class than in many of the "normal" classes of the BIA or the Bethel State school.

The teacher clearly stated that self-expression and communication were the goals of her class and that learning to speak English by mechanical phonetic training was not necessarily the most ideal goal accomplishment of her effort. "I want my children to enjoy communication in any medium they can develop." We will look at the class in this frame of reference.

The room is informally broken up into activity-task areas, where children are pasting, coloring letters, drawing, writing, playing teacher-student in mini-study groups, mastering and using the filmstrip projector, or nursing a sick doll in a crib. The impression is that deaf Eskimo children are the most expressive, communicating, high-spirited children in the Bethel school. We go back to Head Start in Kwethluk to find such free-style, uninhibited interaction. As one researcher notes, "Expressive class with each child handling his own space and learning dexterity with equipment; a very human class with a young female teacher never *in the way* but *available to show the way."*

Why must we go to a deaf class to find uninhibited outgoing Eskimo children? Their abilities appear not to be the *result* of education, but flowering because there was no formal education. Indeed, child for child they *appeared* more outgoing and intelligent, and to be creatively *using* their intelligence.

It was reported that in one deaf Special Ed class a teacher went on brief maternity leave, and the reason for the teacher's absence was explained to the class. At once the class stopped all other pursuits and tended to the birth of the teacher's baby. A doll was stuffed under a student's skirt, she was laid on the floor, birth contractions began, and the baby was delivered. Nothing backward about these kids!

The students meet the teacher's goals. They are fulfilled and communicating vividly with one another. They work with the teacher, but are capable of working alone or of teaching each other or studying a phonetic chart under the direction of a fellow student. The teacher works with individual children and with small groups. The sense of instruction primarily seems to be giving momentum to the students and once they are rolling, the teacher moves to another child. Most of the communication is, of course, nonverbal, mixed with cries of pleasure and pain. The ingenuity of signaling must be in itself very educating.

The Retarded Class

The deaf class seemed intent on teaching deaf kids *not* to be handicapped, humanly and intellectually, by their deafness. The retarded class seemed equally intent on erasing the handicap of retardation. A measure of the teacher's success was that, on film, the children do not *appear* retarded. In fact, this class visually expresses more outgoing sensitivity than those in many other classrooms we have filmed in Alaska.

The difference between this class and the class for the deaf is that in the latter there is more push toward objective education in reading, writing, and dexterity. As in the deaf class there is a wide range of age, from first- through third-grade age levels, which means that the teacher moves from an advanced skill level down onto the floor with kindergarten training for younger and severely retarded children.

There is a free flow of communication between students, verbally loud with sounds of glee, satisfaction, and anger, as well as much bodily communication, pulling, pushing, acting out. The teacher communicates verbally in a low tone and only rarely with an order to "stop," "go," or "sit down." Like the teacher in the deaf class, she was there when needed but took a nonaggressive role in the classroom.

The retarded students themselves are more aggressive. There is lots of physical expression, lots of spirited touch, leading and pulling. The class rhythm was subdued at the start, but as the period moved on, activity increased its pace with exuberant action, play and running. Shoes were off; and barefooted or in stocking feet, the children began to flow ever faster around and around the room. The teacher took off *her* shoes and the class became one dancing-and-running community. There was no sign that the teacher tried to control the pace. Rather, she became part of the pace, so that the class was an exhilerating experience, so necessary maybe for these handicapped youngsters.

It is evident that these Special Ed classes are involved in personality development rather than in a learning conformity that stylized most other elementary schools. We ask: What would happen to learning pace if "normal" Bethel classes were as circulating and free as Special Ed? Would more be learned? Would students develop enthusiasm for school and learning? Of course the normal Bethel class contained up to thirty students while the Special Education classes were smaller. But I feel that the deeper difference lay in differing goals of development.

Bethel High School

The style of the Bethel High School is even more relaxed than the elementary school. There are poor, average, and a few outstanding classes—fewer really excellent classes than in elementary, but this is partly compensated for by a general cooperativeness of pleasant survival in the classroom. The often low expertise of the teachers is forgiven by the students, and the often low achievement of the students is equally forgiven by the teachers. Together they create an ideal climate for one type of development. This is true for the 85 percent Eskimo student body, for Eskimo students are given an opportunity to achieve in the White curriculum simply because stress is low and personality well-being and fulfillment high. We stress the *relaxation* because conventionally students in high school have *more* stress physiologically than in elementary school. Adolescent stress is barely visible in the Bethel High School classes. In Anchorage this situation is reversed.

The White students are swept along on this relaxed rhythm but often with benign boredom and only occasionally do they express their distaste for the provincialism of their Eskimo classmates. After all, most of the White students are as impermanent as the rest of the itinerant White population of Bethel. Many have come from academically superior schools and soon will be going out to the dominant school patterns of the "Lower Forty-Eight."

This view is not simply an empirical impression but recognition of fluent visual patterns of behavior. Body relaxation is very general on the part of both students and teachers. Physical movements of the teacher at his desk or away from his desk are casual. Students come in and go out freely. Interpersonal communication *in* classrooms, student to student, is open and uninhibited, and even when interruptive causes no noticeable stress in most teachers. Students ignore lessons and busy themselves at other tasks shamelessly and happily. Even when classes are essentially negative, students sit peacefully. There are few facial signals of irritation, few overt signals of hostility. To us this symbolizes a receptive situation with minimal rejection, which may mean the school has in a nondirectional way developed a hospitable school culture. Is this the result of a studied scheme, a concrete philosophy? Or the result of a series of circumstances ushered together by the environment of Bethel? Certainly there were no bitter competitive ethnic conflicts. Forces conflicting with Eskimo well-being are so vast as to be abstract. The White population, broken down in its five compounds, is fed from *without,* directed from *without.* This makes its interaction in the Bethel community aloof or amused, and by default tolerant. Only the Moravian Church exerts objective pressure on the Bethel Eskimos, and this is barely reflected in the school.

A General Business Class

Mr. Business is representative of the relaxed Bethel High School faculty. I am sure he finds his tour of teaching in Alaska an amusing interlude but one likely to end soon. His cordial manner on film certainly reveals that he likes his students. His manner is leisurely and friendly in the classroom. His curriculum seems well organized and task-oriented, with texts and quizzes on his subject, General Business.

The film opens with Mr. Business seated comfortably talking about transportation and the highway system of California. He likens the California smog created by cars to smoking three packs of cigarettes a day. He gives the statistics of traffic death tolls. "Very heavy accidents take place just twenty-five miles from home." He sketches the function of the American Automobile Association, how to read road maps, how not to park in a tow-away zone—"That will cost you twenty dollars!" Parking is very difficult in the business section. "How much do you suppose people pay to park in a lot for an hour? Ten dollars? Three dollars? Two dollars? Wrong. It costs 25¢ an hour! Now, study the California road map. How many gallons would it take to drive from San Francisco to Los Angeles?" The tape is not entirely clear, but this is the drift.

The research team describes the class as sleepy and half-responding, though some do respond and ask questions. The verbal approach is given with a light touch, and such an approach might go over great with California boys and girls. Amazingly it did move the students to look at road maps, to measure, and to calculate. Mr. Business was a reasonable, communicating, well-meaning teacher. The class accepted him and were unthreatened when they found the subject incomprehensible or just boring. They would simply yawn and converse with each other.

What might have happened in the class if air-miles to Kuskokwim villages, or gas-miles by snowmobile to Napaskiak, to Akiak, or to Akiachak were calculated? Or jet fuel between Bethel and Anchorage, and Anchorage and Seattle?

When Mr. Business stops lecturing, students appear more oriented to the learning task before them. Students group together, compare notes, communicate generally, and then bring papers directly to the teacher. Sometimes three or four students are at his desk. The scene is better. The teacher communicates, and students' faces show renewed interest. Then the class curriculum shifts to mathematics, and the students work from prepared study material, again making occasional journeys to the teacher's desk. The students seem far more involved in the math than in the AAA or roads in California. When Mr. Business demonstrates math on the board the students really give him attention.

General Science and Chemistry: An Eskimo Teacher

Does an Eskimo teacher change the pace of learning in the high school? Bethel High had one Eskimo teacher, a native of Bethel. Mr. Native is a smartly dressed slender man, looking very un-Eskimo in his business suit, dark-rimmed glasses and crew cut.

In his ninth-grade General Science class, Mr. Native sits at the head of a long table. One White girl, one Eskimo boy, and four Eskimo girls are grouped around the table as if in a seminar. Ten feet away is a second table with two White boys and one Eskimo boy. They appear detached from the activities of the larger group. The teacher reads from a text, first seated, then leaning over the book and resting on his arms, and finally stand, book in hand, as if addressing himself to the whole room.

The tape records Mr. Native reading monotonously from a text on vulcanology. As one researcher noted, he read "all the big words distinctly but as if he didn't understand them." Mr. Native was a university man, but he did have difficulty making this text alive, since he was just reading it. Lack of intonation and expressive pace made the text hard to understand, but each student was reading from his own identical text, as if the learning were putting the book to memory. After a bit, the students read in turn from the text in the monotonous manner so common in obligatory text recitation. Only the White girl appeared to relate to the subject matter and, with fluid hand gestures, enlarge on the account. No one else in the class had anything to add beyond the letter of the text, or any feeling to release about the creation of the earth. However, this is a universal theme, and certainly Eskimos have legends of creation, too.

At the other table *all* the boys are fashioning large drawings that consume the whole class period. Is the subject matter related to the class subject, or are they just doodling? At one point, one of the boys also reads aloud from *his* text, but on finishing returns to his drawing. Mr. Native walks over and observes the activities, asks a few questions, and returns to his seminar group. He seems unconcerned *what* is going on at the table with one Eskimo and two White boys.

Three times the teacher left the room abruptly, and there was a slight change in behavior: more talking together and the like. One of the boys who was drawing shouted across to the long table. Suddenly the teacher returned. Again there was little change. Noise tapered off slowly into the leisurely, contained pace that characterized this class and possibly many classes in Bethel High.

Data sheets on this class are confusing. There was a question as to what *really* was happening. Researchers are not in agreement over the function of the class.

A second film, of Mr. Native teaching a tenth-grade chemistry class, is also enigmatic. One data sheet states, "This is an elite class that needs the barest of direction." Another: "Motivated to study because they need this course to get into college." Compared to the general science class, we see many of the same features. The students relate to their teacher humanly, and are disciplined in their behavior. But Mr. Native gives very little of himself. There seems a wall of quiet around the teacher that is hard to penetrate.

The film opens on what is essentially a study period. Students are writing up notes and personally asking the teacher about elements of their written assignments. There are three groups, two standing clustered around circular laboratory stands and one—a group of four girls—working at a table. There are two White boys at the central table and one White girl. Mr. Native is at his desk looking through papers. The students are all quietly involved in their tasks, writing in their notebooks, discussing freely with one another, presumably talking about the experiments. One writes, moves to the teacher's desk, and talks a long time with the teacher. An Eskimo boy joins him. The teacher follows the White boy back to his table, moves on over to the four girls, briefly pauses, and returns to his desk.

Now the teacher leaves the room again and a level of free association begins to develop. The girls at the table begin talking animatedly *not* about chemistry. The boys at the table move around, and a very relaxed and social air filled the room. The teacher returns, but the general animation continues. Mr. Native smiles on the students sympathetically, opens a text book for a questioning student, and the repetitious round of behavior continues to the end of the session.

Considering our proposition that education takes place within communication, both of Mr. Native's classes had free-flowing student-to-student communication. And certainly the boys' free drawing could have been a communication with self. Hence, one level of education could have been going well in these classes. Mr. Native did free the classes for their own style of involvement. But what did the teacher contribute beyond this freedom? On film we observed no intense one-to-many or one-to-one teacher communication, as was observed so richly in Mr Scout's second-grade class. There did not appear to be any special social relationship between Mr. Native and his Eskimo students. In fact, his longest communication was with a White student.

Possibly Mr. Native was very self-conscious at being filmed, though there seemed to be little change in his general mien before and after the filming. Close study of the film reveals a certain ambivalence, possibly relating to his role as a Native-born Eskimo teacher instructing in his own hometown. Mr. Native did not renew his contract in Bethel and sought assignment elsewhere. In our conclusions we will consider further this phenomenon of the "Native teacher."

Beyond the teacher's performance, we have an equally significant performance of ninth- and tenth-grade Eskimo and White students interacting with one another.

There was literally little difference among these ethnic groups. Eskimo and White blended together in one classroom culture, which further illustrates the openness of the Bethel High School, where Eskimo pace appeared to dominate the atmosphere.

Two English Classes

Miss Vista teaches freshman English, Mr. Poet teaches tenth-grade English. Between them they span a wide range of teaching styles in the Bethel High School.

Miss Vista had come to the Kuskokwim for VISTA and spent a year at the tundra village of Akiachak. When her tour of duty was over, she accepted a job at Bethel High. Her class was held in the same room as that of General Business, which is set up for teaching typing and not for a circulating classroom with flowing interpersonal communication.

The film opens with Miss Vista talking by her desk to a subdued classroom. Her theme: *Words*—what they are and how to use them. Students are directed to create dramas in the class to check the use of words. "Give your attention to the people acting just the way you would like them to listen to you!"

With this introduction there is much moving around, students forming a group in a corner, and the general behavior of the class changes radically. Students sit forward. Eyes are brought in focus, and there is a sense of expectancy. A series of dramas unfold—rather wild, much running in from the wings, as it were, and hilarious responses from the class. Miss Vista takes a stand to one side of the class, as if turning the period over to the students. Her communications are lowered to a direction here and there, whereas student-to-student communication greatly increases. The students were nonverbally grasping the conceptual verbal character of words, probably an approach that should have been used in first and second grade. The class has five or more White students, and they appear equally drawn into the learning action. Had a year in Akiachak village sharpened Miss Vista's approach? Later we filmed a large grammar class in Anchorage where *no one* was drawn into the learning action.

In contrast to this class is the tenth-grade English class taught by Mr. Poetry. Figuratively, and perhaps actually, this is a film revealing the gap between the White teacher and the Eskimo students. The striking character of this class is its use of space. The teacher sits alone on a chair at the front of the room. Two Eskimo girls sit alone in the far left corner. Two Eskimo boys and one White boy sit centrally in the back. Two White boys and one Eskimo sit by the window on the far right. Thus, *all* the eight students are seated against the wall at the *back* of the room or directly along the window at one side. "Sitting by the windows," we have observed in Bethel and elsewhere, is one way to withdraw, as if *out* the window.

Here is a class with only eight students, a small, conversational, group opportunity. But the teacher's approach to the space is as if he had a large class sitting in the rows of empty chairs. Is he unaware that he had only eight students? Is the small group a challenge that can be avoided here only by retaining a safety belt of space between himself and his students? Whatever the reason, what appears as an elite, small, upper-class seminar is run like a large, impersonal class.

The subject of discussion is the symbolic meaning of an English poem—a proper seminar subject—over the 20-foot gap of the empty chairs. Questions are not directed to individuals but toward all the empty chairs. Intimacy of communication is avoided completely. The film records very little communication from the class. The tape records responses given, but apparently these are given so impersonally as to be almost invisible on the film. The two Eskimo girls are silent throughout. One Eskimo boy in the middle communicates visibly. One White boy by the window communicates visibly. Interaction in the class is a racial balance of boredom.

The Reprobate Teacher

The Bethel High School had its rebel, Mr. Flash, the bearded Algebra teacher. Mr. Flash came from the "Lower Forty-Eight" charged with rebellion and at once sand-bagged his classroom, ready for attack. The principal of the high school was a disciplined, orderly man who liked *control*. Mr. Flash disrupted the calm of the principal's life. Mr. Flash despised the compounds and lived by the river with a VISTA worker; his quarters were frequently full of both Eskimo and White students.

Mr. Flash believes in total educational freedom and considers the Bethel High School a prison destroying young minds. Flash set forth to free the prisoners. I am sure the school superintendent also was upset by Flash's war on education, but he harbored as well a secret admiration for dissent and always stopped short of firing him.

Here was Summerhill on the Kuskokwim. What could the most revolutionary educational approach do for the Eskimo student? Mr. Flash runs his classroom on a one-to-one level. He despises lecturing in any form and feels students should be free to reject the curriculum at any time and leave the room. *No* attendance is asked. All that he seeks from his students is *integrity* of self-possession.

The film opens on a class predominantly Eskimo. Fifteen students are scattered about the room, hunched over papers and books. Mr. Flash is demonstrating a mathematical process to interested students, his back turned to the class at large. During this chalk-talk, three students get up and leave the room after signing their names on the blackboard. They have left for study in the library. Now Mr. Flash leaves the board and leans over a lone Eskimo working on a problem at his desk. The communication is intense. In the meantime more students sign their names and leave.

Now Mr. Flash moves over to a group by the window, and the camera records the most intense teacher-to-student communication in the whole high school sample. Students are equally communicating with the teacher *and the conversation is totally about mathematics.* More students leave for the library. Finally the room is half empty, but those who are left are *not* gossiping with one another but are wholly and *individually* absorbed in algebra.

Surprisingly Mr. Flash turns out to be classical in his approach to his subject, mathematics, and he communicates this field with enthusiasm to his students. *But all communications are about math.* After from half to two thirds of his students have been cleared out, the camera records the most subject-involved, intense class in the school. Communication from the teacher is on an intensely personal level and mature in content. He *expects* his students to be turned on by algebra, and those who stay *are*. One of our data sheets reads, "The teacher is into math, and the students are going into it too." The teacher's concentration and interest in his subject have this effect. Students have freedom, but with a purpose—as traditional as this may sound.

Apparently the students do respond to motivation. Mr. Flash carried the students *beyond* relaxation, and a few genuinely accepted the disciplined challenge of mathematics. But Mr. Flash was not rehired for the next year. . . .

Postscript: A Visit of Students from St. Mary's High School on the Yukon

One educational event gave perspective on the Bethel High School and helped define both its weakness and its potential. This event was the homeward-bound visit of a group of high school seniors from St. Mary's High School, fifteen air-minutes west of Bethel on the lower Yukon.

St. Mary's is a Catholic school with about a hundred students and has been established for some time, but in the last few years it has apparently undergone major changes that are having reverberations in the Eskimo community of Bethel. The best Native dancers traditionally come from the Yukon, and the area is spoken of as having a special vitality of Eskimo culture. A French Franciscan priest recently took over the superintendency of St. Mary's, and whether it was because of the high cultural vitality of the Yukon or because this priest realized the value of increasing Native cultural energy, the school was reorganized *around* Eskimo cultural determination.

Maybe there is a conflict and competition here in religious proselytization and zeal by differing groups, such as is seen in our southwestern states, where the Catholic Church sees its anchor to be in Indian ceremonialism, in opposition to the more fundamentalist Protestant groups who feel *all* Indian religious culture is heathenish and the tool of the devil. The Moravian missions made a strong stand on this latter belief and have largely stamped out Native ceremonial culture in the Kuskokwim villages. The Catholic priest saw zeal and religious strength in Native culture and proceeded to introduce bilingualism and biculturalism into his school. Eskimo dancing was *taught* in the high school by Native teachers. Anthropology was taught on all grade levels through assistance from the University of Alaska.

Now the St. Mary's seniors came to Bethel to entertain the Bethel High School classes. The event was the triumphal return of the senior class from a visit to Juneau, where they had danced for the governor of Alaska. Their visit to Bethel was to give an account of this cultural mission to educate the governor in the cultural vitality of the Yukon Eskimos.

The film opens on a double classroom that is commonly used for such large gatherings. Every high school student is there, White and Eskimo, and all the high school teachers are there to note the progress of the St. Mary's students. The first observation shows that White students are sitting in a loose group to one side. The rest of the room is occupied by Eskimo students, while the teachers stand by the doors. The St. Mary's students are seated around one long table near the window; there is considerable open space around them that puts them "on stage."

One by one, speaking through a mike, the students address the whole assembly in clear, spirited English with accounts that send the Bethel Eskimos into roars of laughter and bring mystified looks to many of the Bethel teachers. As one teacher was heard to say, "These kids have had an education! We can't get our boys to speak like that!" Both boys and girls from St. Mary's spoke out fluently with beaming and confident faces. The miracle of education has come to Bethel, and apparently we are seeing the practical effects of a culturally determined school that is trying to *build* on the very foundations that the Kuskokwim schools are either *ignoring,* educating *away from* or educating *against.*

This occasion also measured the results of a culturally relevant curriculum. While the Bethel Eskimo seniors were responding so positively to the St. Mary's students, the few White students formed a bored clique. There were aggressive signals of rejection, yawns, hand signals of distaste, and open ignoring of the program by reading American hot-rod magazines.

THE PUBLIC SCHOOLS OF ANCHORAGE

The flight from Bethel to Anchorage is two hours by jet. As the plane circled away from Bethel, brown tundra was breaking through the thawed May snowpack. The river was nearly clear of ice in channels of black water. But the mountains southward that wall in the Kuskokwim watershed were still locked in the Arctic winter. The journey eastward was over hundreds of miles of Alaska wilderness, for the most part empty of human life, and this wilderness made the city of Anchorage on Cook Inlet shocking in its vast spread of roads and squared property. As we settled into the airport, the White man's world blotted out the North.

Anchorage is spoken of as the largest Native village in Alaska, but it is a White man's city, almost completely removed from the Arctic. It contains an effectual public school system with Native children comprising 7 percent of the student body. These figures are deceptive, for some schools in Anchorage have *no* Native children at all, and many White youngsters grow up here with no contact with Indians, Aleuts, or Eskimos. The Superintendent of Elementary Education was not happy with the Native education in the schools. "We believe only a portion of the Native children are in school. Many children are not even registered. School is so painful to some Native children that they simply stop coming."

With this discouraging introduction we set out to film the same sample as in the Bethel school: from kindergarten through to tenth grade, with a recording of one Special Education class for the deaf.

Kindergarten

In the Head Start class in Kwethluk we filmed a unity and growth in togetherness. In Bethel we filmed compulsive efforts to command learning in kindergarten. In Anchorage we filmed the professionalism of a well-trained teacher conducting a programmed kindergarten where children were directed and gently manipulated into education.

The film opens on a noisy, visually happy kindergarten class scattered around a quadrangle of low tables in a bright, large, well-equipped room—"an enlarged playhouse," as one researcher noted. The class included four Native children—an Eskimo boy, an Indian boy, and two part-Indian girls who looked more Latin than Indian—plus one Black boy, and twelve very White boys and girls.

The teacher in a clear, attractive voice brings order and calls the roll—an innovation in our Alaskan experience. Then a girl student stands holding the American flag, the class pledges allegiance and sings "My country, 'tis of thee . . .," and we know we are back in the United States.

Control, order, and direction set this kindergarten apart from all the other early childhood classes. How does this affect the Native students? The Eskimo boy grins with usual Eskimo enthusiasm. The Indian boy sits wrapped inside himself, docile and obedient. The part-Indian girls seem absorbed into the White community.

The film shows students who keep their seats. There is little wandering around, except for one loner. He drifts off by himself to play house. The teacher moves from one program to another, sing songs about left hand and right hand, and conducts dance games to nursery rhymes she calls out. Students stand on their chairs, revolve their arms, stand on the floor, and wave their arms like birds. Work sheets are passed out. Students begin working with discipline and enthusiasm.

The Eskimo boy stops smiling and begins yawning and turning away from his tasks. The Indian boy is sitting alone in space, no one sitting by him. He smiles feebly, watching others for direction, and finally dropping off, pillows his head on his arms and remains very still. The part-Indian girls also appear out of the group now, one down at the end of a table sitting alone, one centrally seated close to the one Black boy. The Black boy makes many overtures and, not getting reception, begins to bother the part-Indian girl.

Now a group of White children are all sitting together on one side of the table quadrangle with the Eskimo boy seated in their center. In the first part of the filming he seems to be fitting in, works vigorously at his work sheet, and attracts the attention of the teacher. But the longer the class continues, the quieter he becomes. A nursery melody is put on the record player. It is time for recess, and everyone lines up at the door in the conventional, separate, male-female lines.

The film of free-play outside reveals more structured behavior. At first the Eskimo boy is working in the sand hole with four White children. But soon he leaves of his own accord and turns to single play—carrying and throwing large rocks, balancing over a series of planks placed over dried up mud holes. The Indian boy changes his manner entirely. Outside he is still a loner but aggressive, running, chasing White children, finally manually capturing a White girl and forcibly dragging her out of sight around a building wall.

This well-run kindergarten can hardly be called a painful experience for Native children. Yet the two Native boys do express an apartness and behavior that is lonely. The part-Indian girls also were *not* a part of the larger group. It was amazing to see just the same nursery rhyme gestures that we had seen performed in a small, emotionally related, body-touching group in Kwethluk Head Start acted out here regimentally by all seventeen students. Here was the conforming style of the urban and suburban school. Would the Native children adjust and learn in this different environment?

First Grade

Native children were less visible in first grade than they were in kindergarten. Were they adjusting to the dominant class culture the way White children adjusted to the dominant Eskimo culture in Bethel? Only one Native student appeared having difficulties, and the two Indian girls in the room were ranked as high achievers.

This is a large first grade, twenty-five students taught by an elderly, white-haired woman assisted by a young female aide. There are six Natives in the class—one Eskimo boy, three Indian boys, and two Indian girls. One of the Indian boys is visibly withdrawn from the class, never leaving his desk and unresponsive to communications from seatmates. He is ranked by the teacher as an average student. The Eskimo boy and an Indian boy seated near him are both ranked low by the teacher, but their behavior is neutral—relaxed and outgoing. We assume that personality problems are submerged in first grade, probably also in second and third, and barely visible in fifth grade, as student problems take on definition.

This first grade is a programmed, well-run class, held in order by the professionalism of a seasoned teacher, and it is a class which could have further leveled any behavioral differences. This white-haired teacher gathers her flock around her with much impersonal coaxing, comforting, and habitual gestures of affection. She works with small groups, as does her aide, in reading exercises. The children respond dutifully and attentively, but her teaching is not as directional as in Bethel first grades, and little effort is made to draw out individual students. One gets the impression that there is more order but less learning than observed in Mrs. Artist's first grade class in Bethel, and compared with Mr. Scout's second grade this class is just passing time.

Except for the one withdrawn Indian boy, students do circulate freely around the room to join the reading groups of both teachers, but they always return to their seats with minimal interaction with their classmates. Teacher-to-student communications seem to blow over the heads of the class without focus. Behavior is wriggly and full of daydreaming, though one Indian girl is visibly involved, penciling pages, leafing through books, comparing notes with her seatmates—behavior which stands out in this class. This alert Indian girl appears not to be getting any social attention but is just turning on by herself.

Fifth Grade

There were seven Natives in this class of twenty-seven students taught by a motivated male teacher assisted by an uncommunicating female. This room had the congestion one might expect in a city classroom. The class was divided and operated oppositionally by the projections of the two teachers' personalities. The male teacher was seated on a high stool by the windows, encircled by students sitting at desks, on desks, and in chairs. He appeared to draw his students to him, whereas the female teacher sat stolidly at the front of her desk-seated students and never moved through the filming, nor did students go to her. As identified on the seating diagram, three of the Native students were in the assistant's section and four, and one Black boy, in the main teacher's section. But circumstances had moved students around so that most of the Native students were in the head teacher's group, and only two Natives in the assistant's section.

We have not identified what the assistant was presenting, but the male teacher was reading the geography of Colorado. The routine was similar to Mr. Native's General Science class in Bethel. The teacher read from the text and the students read in turn.

Native students sat close to the male teacher, and there was intense eye contact throughout the lesson. The male teacher returned the eye contact, so that there was a strong sense of intragroup relating. After a few minutes the group opened, desks were reoccupied, and the teacher circulated among the individual students, leaning over and sitting by them in person-to-person instruction. He worked intensely with various Native students and a long time with the Black boy in a circumstance reminiscent of Mr. Scout in the second grade in Bethel. But the teacher was harassed. The class was too big, and many students did not get attention. The teacher was concerned, as if he knew he was unable to give the help that was truly needed. Native children knew the head teacher had a listening ear, and there was almost a pathetic eagerness on their part to be heard.

The female assistant gave no visible support to students, and there was the conventional gulf between teacher and class. Here the two Native students responded very differently. The Native boy goofed and clowned. The alert Native girl tried to keep in touch, follow the lesson, and keep cool. The White girls around her appeared to accept her. She looked smart, was well dressed and attractive. The Native boy was ignored.

Generally we were impressed how Native children were fitting into the White urban classrooms. But we asked this same question in relation to White students in Bethel—how did they adjust without stress to the dominant Eskimo pace? The White pace in Anchorage in turn dominated the Native students, swept them along in the elementry grades. But was this apparent adjustment obscuring problems that might have to be faced later in circumstances more difficult than first and fifth grade?

The Native Parent as Teacher in the White School

The principal of this elementary school appeared sophisticated about the challenge facing his Native students, but the school system had no special programs to alleviate this stress. Teachers faced these problems on their own, for help was not offered.

A St. Lawrence Island woman had a son in second grade, and in a gesture of welcome, the principal asked this mother to show her collection of color snapshots and tell the class about life on the islands. Here was a chance to see the response to a Native teaching about a truly relevant Alaskan subject, one of the more isolated Eskimo communities just 30 miles across the Bering Sea from Russia.

The "picture talk" was held in a series of small groups around a table. In this session the principal, a White boy, the Eskimo mother, and an Indian boy sat on one side. At the head of the table sat one more White boy, and across from the mother sat an Indian girl, a Black boy, the mother's little boy, and another Eskimo boy. The woman had a quiet assured verbal delivery and passed the photographs around slowly, explaining each picture in detail.

The pattern of response was surprising. Reasonably the two Eskimo boys really turned on when together they pored over the snapshots. But the next most involved was the Black boy. He looked very intently at each picture, and at one point his eyes opened wide with wonder. The Indian girl showed perfunctory interest. The White boy at the head of the table showed flashes of interest, then sagged into real boredom. The Indian boy looked intently at the pictures, but frowned and looked depressed and weary. The White boy by the principal handled the pictures but showed no interest.

As a teacher the Eskimo woman was unflagging, thorough, and attentive to each student with focused eye attention as she talked. She set a voice and body rhythm and retained it to the end of the filming. She gave special attention to the White boys, as if *they* were the culturally deprived ones who deserved special attention. She leaned toward them, speaking and projecting to them with hand motion and eye focus. She demonstrated that a Native teacher *can* do a controlled clear empathetic assignment in teaching that matches and even betters many professional teachers in the schools.

Did this lesson relate to and support the Native students? It certainly did the two Eskimos. It amazed the Black child (as another "Native"). It moved the Indian boy but puzzled him. It did not appreciably affect the White students, though it certainly informed them.

But the learning situation was excellent—casual, clear, unhurried, and highly personified—and ideal for the disoriented Native student. It is true there was no feedback from the students, except for nonverbal signalling between the two Eskimo boys, but there could have been and would have been, had the teacher shifted her approach. For the Eskimo guest was conventionally aggressive in her style, probably just like some White teacher on St. Lawrence Island. She did not pause long enough in her lecture type presentation for students to express their feelings. After the chaos of crowded and confused students this was still a rewarding moment of relaxed education.

Special Education: A Deaf Class

The culture of education changes abruptly when one enters a Special Education class. In many ways, in terms of Native children, education *begins*. Here teachers deal *directly* with children. Each student's problem becomes the focus of curriculum, and the goals of learning seem directed toward giving confidence and fluency to each child. The goal appears personality fulfillment rather than reaching a conformity of skills. This was as true in the Anchorage Special Ed classes for the deaf as it was in Bethel. We filmed a small class of six students—a Black boy, a White girl, a White boy, and three Indian boys, all between ten and twelve. The White girl appeared to have special problems; she sat smilingly by herself. The rest interacted together in ways very similar to the Bethel deaf class, though this was a more advanced group.

Film opens on a middle-aged White woman communicating orally and nonverbally with a responsive circle of five children gathered around an overhead projector. The lesson is a painfully intense group effort in communication, where students *try* to move from written symbols to understanding verbal meanings in spoken words. There is no representational material to verbalize around. The teacher asks simple questions, as recorded on tape:

T: What is cooked on the stove?
S: Daddy cooks.

This staggered verbal probing is buttressed by fluent hand talk that is exchanged between all the students.

S: Cook—da.
T: Yes, finished.
S: Cooked.
T: Johnny, what does he cook? What?
Johnny: Feetsh!
T: Fish.

The staggered, nearly blocked communication of the tape is not reflected on the film. Here we see a class communicating intensely to the teacher and with each other. Visually this class signals more intragroup communion than any other class in Anchorage, and with high enthusiasm. The students are asked verbal questions. They try to answer verbally, then write verbal answers legibly on the transparent overhead slate, and read their projected writing. This draws in the concentration of the whole class.

We cannot really judge the sense of the questions and answers because so much interlocking meaning is hand talk and general nonverbal communication. But it is our hunch that curriculum is minimal and skill in speech therapy very high. The teacher is very motivating in her efforts to help the students speak and communicate verbally. But as in Bethel this enthusiasm is directed more intensely toward the abstract goal of *communication* rather than toward particular goals *within* communication. Method is to focus learning *directly* on the individual rather than generally to the class, and the result is that students with grave problems are enthusiastic learners.

In this learning environment there were *no differences* between Native and White or Black students. Their common hardships and equal class recognition welded them into one close group. The research team all rated this class the most educationally fulfilling class in Anchorage.

Junior High School: Eighth Grade Math

Education changes severely between fifth grade in elementary and eighth grade in junior high. The fifth-grade teacher taught individuals. Even within the overcrowded chaos he made a great effort to retain a teacher-to-student relationship.

The opening film of eighth grade is a shock. Class size has grown to eighty-five students. The teacher no longer sits with his students but *stands on a platform above them.* He is speaking to the class crowd, never to an individual. Communication is verbal or nonverbal by blackboard demonstration. There is no teacher-to-student eye communication, rarely any student-to-student communication. Everyone seems well disciplined to watch the board and to listen. Somewhere between fifth grade and eighth grade, classroom culture has changed completely.

The film opens with an alert, verbally fluent young teacher lecturing from a raised dais. He turns from notes to writing figures on the blackboard—answers to problems from a past lesson. Then he introduces the next challenge—mathematical probability. He outlines a series of problems, and then gives the class time to work them out. At one point he interrupts his lecture to say, "You kids in the back of the room, quiet down!"

The final high point of the session is a practical demonstration of probability, with each of the students tossing coins and recording the heads-or-tails results. The class suddenly springs to life, with students tossing coins wildly. The teacher interjects, "You don't have to flip them up to the ceiling to get results!" The teacher leaves the front of the room and watches the class from his desk located at one side of the room, and the students settle down to compute probability.

There are eight Natives scattered through this large class. In the early minutes of film all of them seem adjusting to this impersonal circumstance. There is no appreciable difference in their behavior, though the camera was unable to record clearly some of these students. One Native student did stand out immediately because of an extremely self-conscious manner. He was listening, but at the same time showed anxiety with a stiff posture and eyes that looked searchingly about him, as if in confusion or distraction.

General class behavior with the beginning of the coin tossing was social with joking and goofing. But as the problem deepened, students became increasingly absorbed. Heads dropped lower and body positions shifted to postures of absorbed thought and quandry. The Native students held on with no visible signs of lagging, *except* for the Indian boy at the back of the room. *His* head dropped lower and lower. His pencil hand was moving. He was struggling. Now his head dropped *all the way in his arms* and stayed there a long time. When he straightened there was a noticeable change in expression. His face was angry, and after a bit his head sank down on his desk again.

A White boy next to this Indian at the far back of the room presented an extreme contrast in study behavior. This student had pushed his desk out and propped his feet up on another empty desk and settled himself in a half-reclining position, designed to give both comfort and a more absorbing approach to his copybook problem. He chewed his pencil, erased, chewed, scribbled, and gave an appearance of enthusiastic absorbtion with his mathematical riddle.

The Indian boy sat rigidly, not enjoying the situation, and when he did participate, it was with extreme effort as his body signaled slow defeat, finally sinking completely down on his desk. Indeed, this is a sample of one, but maybe it does describe *how* a Native student gives up.

Ninth Grade English

Ninth grade was held in the same room as eighth grade. It was appreciably smaller, about fifty-five students. Even more importantly, the challenge was very different. This class was not the intensely achieving circumstance that was observed in eighth-grade math. The subject was a technical review in grammatical construction and was demonstrational with a lowered demand on both concentration and cognition.

Film opens with the teacher not on a dias but speaking from a podium on the floor. This was not the regular teacher. The challenge for the class is chalked on the board: "The umpire insisting that his eye sight was excellent declined to reverse his decision"—this to be punctuated, requiring an analysis of the various modifying words, phrases, and clauses. The teacher proceeds to ask questions about the sentence structure. There are answers from the floor and lots of apparent note taking.

A second challenge: "The filling mashed potatoes soaked in olive oil was not very tasty" More questions and answers, though this one was more complicated. It would appear that if your English had a weak structural background this lesson would have very little significance. On film the subject had little significance to anyone. Hence there was a general distraction and shared boredom that made recognition of Native behavior difficult.

But there were patterns in the room. The fifteen Native students were bunched together in twos and threes with at least two Natives sitting alone in the midst of White students. Native behavior was goofing around. Two Indian boys in the front row were handling the circumstance humorously, sharing jokes with their nearby White companions. Two Native girls in the far back rows conversed with each other, appeared as nonparticipants, and remained aloof from *their* surrounding White schoolmates. One Indian boy near the front on the far right responded with frowns that could be interpreted both as stress and disapproval, but doggedly held onto the lesson and was one of the most applied members of the class. A lone Indian girl dutifully made notes and listened intently with a calm look that might mean tolerance as well as boredom. At the end of the class time she walked slowly through the room with composure and dignity, avoiding and ignoring the students around her.

The teacher pushed his traditional grammar lesson hard and responded, when kids were overtly misbehaving, "I would like you to move up next to Momont, Mr. Christiansen, so you won't have to worry about what's going on outside!" At other times when responding or asking questions he called students by first name. In both classes teachers were laboring under established school culture, class size, and curriculum. They taught intensely but in the case of the grammar lesson, with futility. Nevertheless, these were typical circumstances that Native children must face when leaving the villages for congested city schools.

High School: Tenth Grade History

This was the end of our sample curve and our final opportunity to observe the welfare of Native students in White schools. The tenth grade was as contrasting to junior high as eighth grade was to elementary school, and offered us new perspectives. This tenth-grade world history class was held in the smallest room filmed anywhere in our survey, 30 feet by 30 feet, with an unusually small class of six Native and nine White students. There were two Indian girls and four Indian boys; the remainder were male Caucasians.

The teacher was friendly, outgoing, and self-confident and appeared responsive to her students. The subject of discussion was the Second World War. This should have been a conversational class, but it seemed to fall into the conventions already established in the schools at large: the teacher speaker, the student listener—despite efforts made to overcome this convention.

The film opens with a pleasant faced middle-aged woman standing in front of her desk answering students' questions about the ending of the film they had been showed the day before.

"What happened at the end?"

"You mean yesterday?"

"Yeh."

"Well, the British continued to resist. They didn't give up. . . ."

By size and seating this class is ideal for give-and-take conversation. It is a question and answer class, and the tape records continuous talk by teacher and students. But when the film is viewed we see some students sitting silently throughout the session. A few vocal White students are doing most of the responding. On film, many hands are raised, wagged enthusiastically, but unrecognized, till arms would drop and bodies settle back into seats. Is the teacher preferential? Or simply unable to handle this rush of two-way communication?

The Indian girls never raised their hands. Many White boys raised theirs, though often they simply spoke without asking. Two Indian boys raised their hands but were not called on. One Indian boy in the front row *did* speak out eloquently without raising *his* hand, but his facial expression was angry, and his physical manner expressed defeat. He shook his head while speaking, then pursed his lips, and dropped his arms leadenly.

Not all the White students were involved. There were individuals who appeared as negative as any of the Indians. It was important that there were White "Natives" as well as Red Natives in this class. The Whites were covert in *their* rejection, with rigid, sometimes angry or simply blank expressions, and gave no visible signs of involvement. Their withdrawal was from school, whereas the Indians' withdrawal was also from the White world that *is* the school; hence their frustration was more bitter.

The Indians began the class with a resigned restraint that the girls carried through to the end. But as the period lengthened the Indian boys' expressed increased discomfort, and their resignation changed to overt resentment. Their manner fitted Harry Wolcott's descriptive concept of the Indian child as a prisoner of war held captive in the classroom (Wolcott 1969). What can a prisoner of war learn from the enemy, the teacher? The Indian boys in the front row did not give up. They did not put their heads down on the desk like the boy in the eighth-grade math class. *Their* withdrawal was anger and militant distaste.

The view of the Anchorage schools gave perspective to the tundra school in Bethel with its relaxed pace and unthreatening curriculum. Intense effort went into the Anchorage high school. The achieving drive, the pressure of crowded space with its dominating White pace could be an extreme hardship for the Native student—and an insurmountable stress for many of them.

Were Native children suffering because of inferior educational foundations? Or were we observing an erosive process more pervasive than the schools themselves? Could education offset this assault on personality? Or was education the fatal agent that brought the destruction? Our thoughts go back to the tundra villages for educational renewal. What might avert the Native failures suggested in the urban school?

6 / Evaluations

WHAT WE HAVE SEEN

Geographically we started by looking at the Eskimo child in his remote village on the tundra where his surroundings and all his associations, apart from school, are Eskimo, and where the ecology and the traditional home and community exert the maximum influence over the emotional and intellectual development of the child. Next, we moved down the Kuskokwim River to the mercantile and administrative center of Bethel where White-dominated economy meets the ecology of Alaska on its own ground, and White and Eskimo lifeways coexist in their prescribed areas. Finally, we moved 400 air-miles east to the modern American city of Anchorage where modern economy and technology serve to insulate the inhabitants from the full brunt of the Arctic, though the economy is still dependent upon the exploitation of this ecology.

Ethnically, the movement is parallel. In the tundra villages the Eskimo child goes to school in the most saturated Native circumstance, where only the school, traditionally an outpost of the BIA, provides a model of the White world. In the town of Bethel Eskimos go to an integrated Native-and-White consolidated state school in a traditionally White school culture. The child grows up seeing both ways and their relation to each other, but in any case, 85 percent of the student body is Eskimo. In Anchorage, Eskimo, Aleut, and Indian children attend a traditional municipal public school system, where these Natives combined make up only 7 percent of the student body. Regardless of the Native population of 5,000, Eskimos here are a tiny minority, living remote from Native culture and ecology, nearly as engulfed in the White life style as they would be in Seattle or Oakland, where school and community are similarly dominated by White values.

In terms of age cycle, we observed Eskimo children coping with White education from Head Start, kindergarten, and prefirst through to tenth grade, with a focus that documents the changing emotional adjustment to challenges of White acculturation that dominate education. We have particularly looked at the changing projection of stress, under different circumstances, of the Bethel school and the Anchorage schools in an effort to determine what is the most fulfilling learning circumstance that can deal with the psychological problems of adolescence in the acculturation and socialization of the Native child. My evaluation will be to examine these three curves of Eskimo development tracked through the twenty hours of film.

The Geographic and Environmental Curve

Children in the elementary school in Kwethluk were more motivated than were the children in Tuluksak, which was relatively a more economically depressed community. But the children of Kwethluk were also more motivated and educationally eager than the school children in the tundra mercantile center of Bethel. In turn the Bethel children were more motivated than the Native children in the elementary school in Anchorage.

Because Bethel *is* an Eskimo trading center and the center of salmon fishing, Eskimo culture ebbs and flows in from the villages up and down the Kuskokwim and nearby areas of the Yukon that offer Eskimo children a cultural environmental base of operation. It is true that the school largely ignored this potential, but it must have accounted for the high level of vitality in *both* elementary school and high school in Bethel. The environmental setting seemed to influence the high school particularly. The older boys raced sled dogs and competed in summer boat racing. Many worked full time, fishing through the summers. Education could well capitalize on these resources that are already quietly adding to the well-being of the Bethel school.

We can conclude that small regional schools can offer a more fulfilling program for Eskimo students than large centers that separate students from renewing a culture that is locked in ecology. St. Mary's Catholic High School may owe much of its durability to its regional setting.

The Ethnic Component

Educators have long been aware that there may be a tipping point in the balance of biracial student bodies, where behavior can change rapidly. Our analysis demonstrated this thesis. In Bethel, where 85 percent of the students were Eskimos, the low stress was directly related to the relaxed pace set by the dominant Eskimo group culture. The high percentage of Eskimos carried the White 15 percent of the student body along with this pace. Even the teacher's behavior may have been meaningfully affected by the Eskimo character of the school culture. This saturation of Eskimo style certainly made education pleasanter and more palatable to the Eskimos and sharply reduced the stress reasonably expected in acculturation, especially in adolescent years.

Anchorage exhibited a painful environment where White pace and values weighed down the Native students and made life intolerable for some in the schools. Eskimos, Indians, and Aleuts are a minority in Alaska and are officially referred to as "the Native problem," a public role that is not one of success. Education has much to gain by working with the Natives' ethnic well-being. There is no evidence that this would slow the educational process. Quite the contrary, a relaxed fulfilled student internalizes and communicates better than the rigid, aching student who has lost his sense of well-being.

The Age-Cycle Curve

Consistently in many minority groups in the "Lower Forty-Eight" (for example, Blacks, Mexican-Americans, Indians), students reach a crisis point in adolescence and high school. This is where the heaviest dropout rate takes place. And here many minority students are facing their first bitter inequality with the dominant society. But in other cultures adolescence is not necessarily a period of inevitable stress.

In Bethel High School, adolescence appeared not to be such an important factor. High school students continued to be relaxed and socially fulfilled in both community and school. There was no dramatic dropout rate as adolescence proceeded.

In Anchorage, as we have stated, this curve was reversed, and Native students conformed to the conventional model. Stress grew higher with each school year. Reasonably, Native adolescents *were* facing the hard realities of being a minority in a White man's world. Many were faced with severe economic insecurities that in Bethel would be borne partly by the extended family culture. Thus, school became a greater challenge, and education, for some, became a humiliation instead of a stimulating fulfillment. Obviously, as we have observed on film, White adolescents were also suffering. But they were White and had the security of White success to pull them through. In terms of age cycles in education, the Native student appears to have a better chance of fulfillment within his own supporting environment and cultural group.

These observations are written about the *present* acculturation process in this phase of American history—*now!* We are speaking of circumstances best adapted to *becoming modern Eskimos*. First we must educate for secure, fulfilled, and resourceful Eskimos. When we accomplish this, the right door to the future will open itself.

No Basic Differences between School Systems

Our key-sort cards gave us a rough statistical comparison of the differences and similarities of Alaskan schools. These indicated that there is basically no difference in the education presented to Eskimo students by the schools, regardless of whether the schools are run by the BIA, by missionaries, by the State of Alaska, or by the Anchorage municipal school system. In working over the film to find areas of similarity and differences, we found consistently that in all areas related to the educational approach and administration—in curriculum, classroom appearance, educational materials and their use, teaching methods, general teacher behavior, and teacher relationship to students—there were no significant differences between systems. Indeed it would be difficult to look at any class in the sample on film and be able to identify it as being BIA, state, or public school. For this reason the research team often exhibited a certain amount of confusion as to which classes were in which system—until they memorized the code numbers on the film boxes. To be sure, within each school system there were different sorts of teachers who approached their students in often widely different ways, but each seemed to exhibit the same range of approaches, with no major difference between systems—only between teachers.

All schools teach the same "White Studies" program. If there are basic faults in Eskimo education, these failures are shared by all of the schools. It is essential to be absolutely clear on this, for many people with varying motives feel that emancipating the Eskimo from the BIA will solve the problem of Native education. This is fallacious and hides the true shape of the problem, which is that White schools in Alaska or elsewhere in the United States have not met the challenge of equal education for the ethnically and culturally different child.

There were fine and dedicated teachers—and ineffectual teachers—in all the schools. The material quality of the schools in Eskimo villages is as good as, if not superior to, that of many rural schools in the "Lower Forty-Eight." The schools on the tundra were, if anything, overequipped. But any superiority was in terms of the materials and needs of American culture, and did not thereby necessarily meet the needs of Eskimo education.

English, reading, and writing are all taught intensely in each school. Teaching skills and methods were familiar and approved; they were "excellent" for the most part in terms of standard American educational practices. If then, the Eskimos were unable to read and speak clear English, it means we must question how appropriate these skills and methods and equipment were for Eskimos in the Arctic.

We did not observe any teaching of English as a second language or any other effort specifically designed to bridge the chasm between the Eskimo and White worlds. There seems to be a maddening formula that the more we "educate" Native children, the more definite become their problems of effectiveness and fluency. None of the school systems in the sample could be said to balance out this negativity. Possibly the articulate St. Mary's seniors visiting Bethel may have been the result of an effort to meet this problem in Native education.

The philosophy of education in all these schools directs the effort toward assimilating the Native child. Nationally schools follow the principle laid down by Theodore Roosevelt that there is no place in American democracy for two languages, two cultures, or two different allegiances. Education for the minority child has always attempted to Americanize him and separate him from his cultural distinctions. We saw nowhere in Alaska any appreciable departure from this philosophy.

The BIA administration in the Kuskokwim suffers with this challenge and worries about Eskimo culture fading. Indeed it would sincerely like to remedy this situation by some variety of "Ethnic Studies," but when faced with action, it has so far backed down. "Why teach about Eskimo culture when it is doomed to be lost?" The Moravian missionary effort simply rejects the issue and vehemently opposes Native culture whenever it competes with White Christian precepts for the Eskimos' faith and allegiance. The state schools supply their libraries with literature on Eskimo history and culture. It is there if the Eskimos wish to read it. Public schools in Anchorage also have ethnic studies texts in their libraries. But these books are looked upon as social studies; for the most part they are directed toward White children, explaining the strange exotic ways of Eskimos—rather than *life studies* for Eskimo personality survival. State schools tend to treat all children "the same," which tends to reinforce the unequal opportunities for Eskimo children.

The BIA schools and teachers are aware they are teaching Eskimos. Therefore, they may be more responsive to dynamic change, if indeed it were ever to be sanctioned. But we fear this will never happen, not until all schools together face the issue of equal personality opportunities for all children.

Self-Depreciative Effects of White Education in the Arctic

In filming the Eskimo villages we were impressed with the block to effective education that the White educational compound imposed on the village's self image. It is clear that the schools, educationally, are supposed to make the villagers look about and attempt to raise the standards of village life. This could be a dynamic influence, but we feel the negative effect of this demonstration on Native life destroys any positive end. Defeat in education for Native children, and more seriously later in their mature activities, produces the weight of self inferiority that saps confidence and resiliency.

The educational presence of White teachers with their White culture—the affluent White style necessary for keeping teachers in their jobs in the village schools, whether BIA or state—creates a serious discrepancy that in itself manufactures deprivation among the Eskimos. Depreciation of self is a serious blow to development; and we feel that this disposition, created by the discrepancy that seems inherent in White education, is one of the major causes of failure in Eskimo education.

Culturally, it seems impossible for White teachers in the villages to live in empathy with the Eskimos they are educating. White teachers often greatly enjoy and even admire Eskimos, but the Eskimos' life style continues to shock them. Thus, in the villages a teacher's visit with Eskimos is conducted in the *teacher's* home and not in an Eskimo's. In Kwethluk, Eskimo children flooded into the teachers' compound—and they were usually welcome—to baby-sit with the teachers' children or just to visit as guests. The wall-to-wall carpeting must have fascinated them, along with the immense size of teachers' homes, and the brilliantly illuminated interiors must have made magazine reading and game playing a real pleasure. But how did these children feel when they walked home over the snow to their own small, dark, very crowded cabins?

What should be the role of the White teacher in the Eskimo community, a role that would motivate students and at the same time not abet their sense of deprivation? We filmed just one teacher who, we felt, had mysteriously mastered this combination of teacher and equal human being. If this role cannot be mastered, teachers instruct over an impossible chasm—a chasm existing between *their* world and the *Eskimo's* world. This is a major cause of the defeat of Native education.

It is impressive that the Peace Corps rules out this material discrepancy whenever it can and places its volunteers in Native villages at the same level and in the same style as Native students. The VISTA workers in Alaska are also required to live on the Eskimo level when working in the villages. In both cases the goal is to reduce the human differences.

Relevant Curriculum in Eskimo Schools

The bitterest criticism of the BIA schools is that they are washing out the Eskimos' personality. If critics were fully informed, the charge would be laid against all schools in the Arctic.

While visiting in Tuluksak, an official of the VISTA program for the Bethel region stated, "There is no relevancy anywhere in the BIA schools. How do you expect kids to learn with a curriculum totally unrelated to their lives?" Later, with pencil and paper in hand, I asked him to detail a relevant curriculum for Eskimo children. His mouth fell open, and he was unable to think of one item. A culturally oriented curriculum that would be taught by White teachers is indeed a challenge to construct in the face of the rapid social change that is sweeping the Arctic. But at the same time there is no denying that the absence of a relevant and culturally supporting curriculum is a major fault in Eskimo education.

Our own records, as we have stated, show very few and sometimes no items in Alaska classrooms that would suggest the schools were not in Ohio. The only consistent Eskimo item we did see was an Alaskan Airlines poster that regularly presents Eskimo portraits. In Tuluksak the gamehunter BIA teacher had a chart of Alaskan furs, and his wife had two models of Eskimo camps, one of which had been made for someone else. At least 99 percent of all exhibited materials in schools were about the "Lower Forty-Eight" states. The only school that encouraged free-style art work was the Head Start school; everywhere else the children colored Mother Goose dittos. In early childhood education the only Eskimo-oriented text was one used in Head Start. In all other schools, BIA, Mission, State, and public, *Mother Goose* was exclusively the White goddess of education, and in the first grade it was *Fun with Dick and Jane.* One first-grade teacher in the state school in Angoon, which is outside of this report, used an approved *Native Alaska Reader.* The only class in any school that studied a standard text *oriented* to their environment was the BIA eighth grade in Kwethluk.

We have just five film examples that record Eskimo students' response to relevant curriculum. The most outstanding demonstration of relevance was Head Start in Kwethluk. Not only were the teachers young women from the village who spoke to the children in Eskimo, but the standard Mother Goose routine had been sufficiently acculturated into Eskimo styles of motion and pantomime, so that the children responded with delight. The young teachers did not restrict reading to Mother Goose, but in addition used picture books and storybooks about Eskimo life to stimulate the children's interest in reading.

The second was Eskimo storytelling in first grade in Tuluksak. The students did respond intensely to this Native opportunity, and it stirs one's imagination concerning any contributions that could be introduced from the villages directly into the classroom. Mrs. Pilot also worked with an Eskimo hunting camp models in an attempt to stimulate language use. Even when questioning by the teacher appeared inappropriate, the model did hold great interest for the young students.

The third example on film was made in the eighth-grade BIA class in Kwethluk. The teacher was relating a standard text on mental health to Eskimo life in

Kwethluk, describing verbally "the cultural deprivation in the Lower Forty-Eight." Though this was essentially a lecture circumstance with only a minimum of student exchange, our film reading describes it as one of the most responsive classes in our sample.

The fourth example on film was the visit of the St. Mary's High School seniors to Bethel. First, as a group they were the most eloquent, effectual, and assured students observed in our study. Second, the Bethel Eskimos responded with intense listening and expressions of enjoyment, whereas the White boys dramatically withdrew in an exhibition of boredom and rejection.

The fifth example was in the elementary school in Anchorage, where an Eskimo mother gave a picture talk on life on St. Lawrence Island. Though the uniqueness of the circumstance seemed confusing to the Indian and White students, the two Eskimo boys did respond openly; more importantly, the film demonstrated the competence of an untrained Native woman to teach, to present Native study material in a general classroom.

We conclude that cultural relevance can appreciably improve reception and projection in the Eskimo student, and that most texts and curricula used in all the schools have difficulty reaching, and often may fail to reach, the Eskimo child.

We feel the issue of relevance in curriculum is an issue related to bilingualism. Both issues are important, not necessarily as means of cultural retention but more importantly, as means of fluency in communication that can allow Native children to conceptualize general educational content.

Native Teachers in Eskimo Schools

We filmed only one credentialed Eskimo teacher in all our sample. Eskimos are used as teacher aides in the BIA village schools but their teaching opportunities are limited.

The Charles K. Ray report on Native Education in Alaska, released in 1959, made no recommendations about Native teachers (pp. 242–243). In the body of the report mention is made of BIA teacher aides, who at that time were considered temporary replacements for qualified White teachers. The Ray report states that unquestionably, Native aides are invaluable for White teachers, but the report also expresses anxiety over their educational ability and stresses the importance of weeding out teachers without training and credentials.

These expressed attitudes are the heart of the dilemma. As expressed by the administrator who asked an advisory school board whether they wanted Eskimo-speaking teachers, "Of course there are no *qualified* Eskimo teachers. . . ." In other words, education itself blocks the development of Eskimo teachers by insisting that to teach you must have a credential.

Native instructors in the Head Start program demonstrated the competence of village teachers to perform on a professional level with minimal training. OEO gave these young women a summer workshop at the University of Alaska which was adequate to make them the most effectual teachers of young children filmed in our Alaska study.

When we asked a leading Eskimo intellectual in Kwethluk what should be added to the village school, he answered, "*I* should be teaching in that school." And what could he teach? "I would teach our boys all the things they cannot learn be-cause they are going to school!" He recognized that the schools were destroying *Eskimo education* essential for survival in the Arctic. Yet the Ray report (1959: 2/3) recommends lengthening the school year, to include camping experience.

If White education had its way, it would absorb the Native child completely in just the same way the BIA historically tried to absorb the Indian child in its program of captive boarding-school education.

Native teachers even *without* college education and credentials in the schools might balance out this alarming destruction of the Native child's grasp on his own life and ecology, and offset the hardship of long hours necessarily required to complete school.

We have no illusions about the simple solution of recruiting Native teachers and organizing educational experiences to correct the racial and cultural imbalance of White education. Stepped-up programs to rush teachers through credential programs might not be a real solution, because teacher training itself can interfere with the effectualness of the Native teacher. We observed that you can train and credential an Eskimo without assuring the result of a teacher who can build the conceptual bridge between the White world and the Eskimo. Too often the college-trained Eskimo comes home a confused and culturally schizoid individual.

Training the Eskimo teacher to return constructively to the village school will require new guidelines and a radically changed philosophical approach to educating the culturally different child. Unless this takes place, the value of the Native teacher is often destroyed by the *White backlash* of conventional teacher training. When this happens, White schools seem to educate Natives to become second-class Amer-icans. The Eskimo teacher returning to the Natives can be a harsher critic of Eskimo ways than the White teacher. We have observed that Native teachers who wish to help their own people often impose the same harsh routine of education as *they* were given in the White man's school, for it is all they know in terms of school education.

The Limitations of White Teachers and White Studies

In both BIA and state schools on the tundra, we observed competent, well-trained teachers giving all their time to educating Eskimos. Were these profession-ally skilled teachers doing appreciably more for the Eskimo children than incompe-tent teachers? The most dedicated teacher can become enmeshed in the web of White education to a point where even his skilled efforts turn off the Native child. This was the most disturbing evidence in our films.

Only one teacher in the state school in Bethel, Mr. Scout, seemed to have freed himself sufficiently to teach the thoroughly White curriculum, while at the same time holding out an empathetic hand to his Eskimo students. We found even the teachers who were best in terms of dedication and training were unwittingly and with missionary zeal educating the Native child *out* of his basic foundations of personality and *into* an educationally manufactured personality that does not sup-port his needs in school or later in life.

Tragically, we felt many teachers sensed this but had no resources to alter the process. This haunting suspicion of failure harassed teachers in both BIA and state schools, and was a factor of the futility affecting teacher endurance in working with Eskimo students.

My impression was that their image of educational success was limited to Natives' becoming modern, civilized men embracing White values and ambitions. Their image of failure was the Native student who goes on being a bush Eskimo, as if remaining *Eskimo* were a mark of educational failure. We talked to no teachers who clearly conceived of their students becoming *modern Eskimos,* standing firmly on their past and perpetuating their values into the future. As Murray Wax observed about White teachers on the Sioux Reservation, "The Indians' furniture was invisible, and in the teachers' eyes they lived in an empty house" (Wax and Wax 1964:15–18).

Critics agree that Eskimos and Indians need *better* education. But there is considerable disagreement as to the *goals* for Native education and the *kind* of educational program that might meet them. We agree with many observers that schools as institutions are destroying Native American life, simply because the content of *schools* limits the scope of *education.* Whether in Alaska or in the American Southwest, we find the same educational circumstance—that the schooling of Native Americans is seriously inadequate not only for survival in the American cities but for survival within the Native environment as well. Yet we also feel that *no* schooling would doom the Eskimos completely, so important are the communication and technical skills available in the White curriculum, and so complex and threatening has been the world surrounding even the most isolated Eskimo village. Eskimo survival depends on new lifemanship in the real world of social and technological change. Our interest together should be to envisage the *kind of education* that would offer Eskimos and Indians in the modern world the important equality of participating as individuals and as groups within the general society and of finding fulfillment within themselves and within their own life styles.

Maybe we can speak with more clarity of the educational needs of the Eskimos than of Native Americans at large. For here we find hunting and fishing people within a relatively unspoiled ecology with major economic opportunities still within their traditional life style. We also see a process taking place that parallels the historic pattern of White education for Indians begun a century ago. And we can reasonably suspect that we are making, as White educators, many of the same mistakes that our predecessors made generations ago. We seem to learn only slowly, if at all, about the dynamics of education for Native peoples.

The Eskimos today face a spoils system dominated by White men and an invasion and exploitation of their property, just as group after group of Native Americans did in the eighteenth and nineteenth centuries and as the Navajos and Hopis do now with the push for coal-generated power. With this history the needs for Eskimo education now are dramatically twofold:

1. To retain and enlarge their environmental opportunity as Eskimos.

2. To obtain the special skills and sophistication to cope with the onslaught of the White world and cultural change in general so that they can avoid being made paupers on their own lands or economic or psychological failures in the industrial cities to the south.

Education toward these ends means learning the skills of their own culture so that they can live providently within their Native environment. But equally they must learn skills and sophistication in order to participate in new technologies. They must meet the White invasion with Eskimo solidarity, economically and politically, or they will effectively be driven from the Arctic completely. Competing with the White world does not mean learning Mother Goose, but it does mean literacy and the ability to speak to and reason with White men who know no other language than English. Eskimos need the fundamental components of a sound White education *plus* a depth knowledge of Eskimo skills and culture, if they are going to be able to deal effectively with White men and their schemes. To accomplish these things they need an education to become *effective Eskimos.*

Eskimos need intense survival training, and *they need it right now.* They must learn to survive when a snowmobile breaks down in the vast tundra wilderness in mid-winter. They also need to survive as competitors with White men, using all the modern skills, so that the Eskimo people will be assured a place in the Alaskan enterprise. If their education fails these needs, it is *mis*-education of the most destructive kind that can only hasten their departure from the land that is their birthright.

GOALS FOR ESKIMO EDUCATION

Goals for what? Effective education? On whose terms are we to evaluate? And by what criteria?

Margaret Nick, Eskimo leader from the village of Nunapitchuk on the Kuskokwin, framed this dilemma for Edward Kennedy and his Senate Subcommittee Hearings on Native Education in Fairbanks in March of 1969:

> . . . This last thing I want to say I consider the most important thing in education. Let's ask ourselves a question. A very important question. *What does education mean?* Who knows the answer? Maybe there's somebody in this room who has a degree in education. Maybe he knows the answer. I don't know. How can I predict how my younger brothers and sisters should be educated?
>
> I'm sure my grandparents didn't know what my mom and dad would have to encounter in life. He [they] didn't know how to educate them. Just like I can't predict how I should educate my children. I can't predict how they should be educated, but one thing I know is, if my children are proud, if my children have identity, if my children know who they are, they'll be able to encounter anything in life. I think this is what education means. Some people say that a man without education might as well be dead. I say, a man without identity, if a man doesn't know who he is, he might as well be dead. This is why it's a must that we include our history and our culture in our schools before we lose it all. We've lost too much already. We have to move. We all know that Indian education should be improved and we've got a lot of ideas about how we should improve our Indian education. Now that we have the information, let's not kick it around like a hot potato. Let's take the hot potato and open it before it gets cold (U.S. Congress 1969).

We must focus on concrete purposes of education or we will be unable to conclude our study functionally. There are at least four objectives involved in the fulfillment of Indian education that we feel must be considered.

1) The traditional goal of Native education as pursued by missionaries and historically by the BIA: *Is education successfully fitting Eskimos into the mainstream of American life?*

This is the oldest and most agreed-upon goal, and is an adaptation of the goal of American education at large. But beyond this traditional goal, and sometimes in contradiction to it, we see three other emerging goals that appear essential for Native peoples to succeed in the contemporary environment:

2) The goal of human opportunity: *Does education fit Eskimos to meet whatever problems life presents with resources and resourcefulness?*
3) The ecological-economic goal: *Does education support and equip Eskimos to survive economically in their Arctic environment?*
4) An emotional-health goal: *Does education stabilize and strengthen Eskimo personality so that Eskimos can stand the stress of life, as all men must, in order to survive in the rapidly changing world?*

It will clarify our conclusions if we first evaluate these basic goals.

If schools were succeeding in *fitting Native Americans into the mainstream of American life,* there would be no need for a National Study of American Indian Education. The fact is that attempts to reach this goal have been largely a failure. Even when Indians have had the best schooling in terms of White education, success in the dominant society has too frequently been low. The special problems that appear to exist in the education of Indians—and of many ethnically different minorities—have largely defeated even the classical goal of academic education. The result is that many Indian students fail to master fluency in English and fail equally to meet day-by-day challenges of protocol and practical survival in the White world.

We should speak here about the rationale supporting the mainstream approach. "Why bother to educate Eskimos for anything other than entering the American mainstream, when it is already impossible for Eskimos to live their traditional life?"

White education for Natives, whether they be Eskimo or Navajo, by curriculum *assumes* that the future of Native peoples is in urban centers of wage-work opportunity. The federal government's recurring termination policies for Indian lands make the same assumption. I say, the Arctic is a fine place for an Eskimo future, as much as it seems to be for eager, opportunistic White men. With balanced economic development the future for Eskimos will be largely in Alaska, and therefore they should be educated to take advantage of this future if they so desire. The continuation of Eskimo identity does not necessarily require living in a traditional style, though for many it might mean living within the Arctic ecology.

A second rationale for mainstream education is, "What good is knowing about Eskimo ways for a Native who will live in Seattle?" In terms of personality, knowing Eskimo ways has nothing necessarily to do with living in the Arctic. We view knowing Eskimo ways as knowing about self and building a strong identity that is essential even for the Native who lives in Seattle. Yazzie Begay, a school board member of the Navajo Rough Rock School, sums up this issue clearly:

We need education for our children so they can hold good jobs and get along with people in the dominant culture. But in getting this education they must not forget who they are and from where their strength comes (Johnson 1968:150).

Another Navajo leader, Ned Hatathali, now president of the Navajo Community College at Many Farms, adds to this:

The Navaho people must re-discover themselves in this fast-moving culture of today—they must know where they came from and who they are in order to know where they are going (Johnson 1968:59).

We present a frame of reference that views effectiveness for Natives in their psychological, as well as their practical vocational, skills in modern life. Our three further educational goals are related to educating the Eskimo not only as a practical outer man, but as a whole and resourceful inner man as well.

This focuses directly on this study's conclusion that education for Natives in Alaska is detracting from the goal of human opportunity rather than increasing this equality. All the schools make a valiant effort to teach Eskimos White skills—to master reading, writing, and arithmetic—but while they offer these learning opportunities with one hand, they undermine the relevance of these attempts with the other. Thus Eskimo students, instead of gaining human equality through education, too often are convinced by education that *their life chances are unequal simply because they are Eskimo,* and nothing takes place in White schools to reinforce their confidence that being Eskimo is a unique opportunity rather than a cultural, ecological, and genetic misfortune. Equal tools do not necessarily make equal men. Equality is primarily a *psychological reality.*

Very few Eskimos gain an improved ecological-economic position through education. There is no focus in schools to train and motivate Eskimos to succeed in their native Alaska. All around them they see White Americans apparently enthusiastic about their own futures in the Arctic; *but for Eskimos all arrows in all school systems point south.* Generally education for Eskimos means *to leave their environment,* which is then rapidly filled by White men *who gain wealth* from the same environment. In all schools the curriculum is void even of appreciation of life in the Arctic. Hence we can say that education is structured so as to empty the Arctic of adjusted, successful Eskimos, since the focus of curriculum is to make them dissatisfied with Arctic life by stressing values that can be obtained *only* by leaving.

As for the *emotional-health goal,* it might be said that missionary schools feel they are educating for mental health by bringing Christianity to the Eskimos. Schools in general feel they are adding to mental health by giving youth new values to strive for, by teaching them hygiene, and by raising the style of Eskimo living. Bacteriological hygiene, higher material living standards, and Christian morality are dubious approaches to health of the spirit, when such education cuts across the roots of Eskimo personality. The most generally observed effect of White education for Native peoples is that it usually achieves alienation. Educators should be aware of this eventuality and try to give back as much as they inadvertently take away. In the case of the Eskimos, this balance seems not forthcoming; and educated Eskimos, like so many educated Indians, often have serious personality problems, alcoholism, and high suicide rates. Included in our sample is just one example of a coordinated sustained effort to strengthen students' psychic well-being. This was the example of the students from the bicultural program of the St. Mary's Catholic high school. These visiting students appeared to have durable personalities that had definitely been strengthened within education.

The conflict over the goals of education is no special fault of the Native schools. It is the basic conflict of American education today. But we feel the time is at hand when attitudes must and will change. And the most important change will come in schools. Teachers *can* be trained now and supported in changing the negative course of education not only for Native Americans but for the whole range of ethnically different children. Quite possibly this change will take place first in the inner city, before it affects the tundra. The challenge is not new. It was faced in the New Deal for Indians under Roosevelt. The effort failed then; perhaps it was too diffuse, too romantic, its purpose misunderstood and not sustained. We feel it can succeed *now*.

INTO THE SHARED FUTURE OF EDUCATION

The Native American is no longer alone in his plight of education. The commonality of educational default, the shared problem of human survival in this industrial age, is of great significance to the solutions of Indian, Eskimo, and Aleut schooling. Basically the problem is shared by Afro-American, Spanish-American, and all children, even White children, who must struggle for survival in personality and uniqueness in American conformity.

The chasm we find in the Eskimo classroom is found in the inner city schools of our major cities. The chasm is there in the Anchorage city schools for both Native and White students. Facing this reality can bring many skills to Native education and help clarify the real problems in Indian schooling because it is a larger problem. If we were able to understand and remedy the defects in Indian education, we might finally be at the core of a significant modern education for everyone. I do not feel we are dealing with the unique survival problem of an Eskimo personality, but with a shared problem of personality development for any child.

The goals of Eskimo education evaluated in this conclusion could relate to the success of any American classroom, including the gatherings in colleges and universities as well. I feel the revolution of education has been taking place around these four points. Look at the first goal: *Is education successfully fitting the student into the mainstream of American life?* This is largely the historical function of schools and still is the major goal of public school education. This refers back to the "melting pot" philosophy of Americanization which was for so long the foundation of public school instruction and at the same time the cause of some of the serious failures in education. Compulsive conformity in the mainstream sets the stage for inequality. Students already *in* the mainstream hold superiority over those who must give up *their* stream to become "Real Americans." In terms of mental health, the "melting pot" process has been the leveler of self and the alienation of the society. There are thoughtful teachers who look on the mainstream of American life as a threat to well-being, rather than an educational accomplishment, and pluck their students from this flood for a more humane destiny.

Are White schools fitting students successfully into American life? Never has there been such a high dropout rate from social and economic functions. Is this a fault of education? Probably it is, but it is also a failure of the society itself to offer human fulfillment to its citizens. We are in a cultural upheaval; burgeoning awareness, expectations, and self-determination are challenging every structure of American life in search of new fulfillments. The dilemma of human need creates an atmosphere in which we proceed with a haunting feeling that education has failed. Where? In the classroom? Is this the failure of teachers? In part, yes! We are haunted by our own inabilities to respond to what we know lies outside the school in the real lives of our students. Should this not be a major consideration of education? There is certainly the awareness that education is *not* meeting the challenge of emerging issues. We worry about Eskimo students, and we can be as deeply concerned for the future of all children for they share many of the same survival dilemmas.

The second variable in our evaluation—*the goal of human opportunity*—is in every challenge of contemporary education. What is human opportunity? Is it making $20,000 a year? There can be little humanity in materially powerful success, yet the drive of public education is to make money and to rise to a higher level by making *more* money. What human opportunity is offered the Eskimo child in the White school? To leave his village and succeed financially in Anchorage or Seattle in a White style? This is the central goal offered, other than Christian ethics, Christianity, reading, writing, arithmetic, and physical hygiene. I would presume human opportunity for an Eskimo would be to excel successfully in the modern world as an Eskimo. I believe this is what we all need to achieve human opportunity—to excel in who we are and to be gratified and recognized as who we are. Human opportunity can be economic, but it is also an intrinsic accomplishment in which humanity is the key to gratification and success.

The culturally determined St. Mary's High School offered its students this gratification in building on the self-esteem of the Eskimo. Do we offer the Afro-American this human opportunity? If so, to what extent? What about the people of Appalachia? Where in our school system are students obtaining these gratifications? Only in the limited syndrome where teacher and students relate on the same empathetic plane of values, where otherwise invisible structures of culture are mutually embraced. Is human opportunity and potential a practical goal of education? It could be if the needs for human opportunity were defined and if the processes of reaching these goals were as varied as the children in each classroom.

Economic and ecological goals of learning are essential in retaining our human relationships to our environment. Survival for Eskimos is deeply involved in how they continue to relate to the Arctic ecology. But we may ask: Is the Navajo Reservation being strip-mined for fuel through the failure of sound economic and ecological education? Navajos learn little in BIA schools to alert their leaders to the ecological suicide of selling their underground power resources to White American power needs, a scheme which will destroy millions of acres of grazing land and deplete an already dwindling water supply. Every Native American group has been pillaged by this same greed. Do White schools teach ecological conservation? Do the schools in New Mexico teach Spanish Americans how they can survive on their own lands? Does the California school system teach the value of recreational space and the survival of its forests? We teach about economic success and mastering nature's resources in terms of dollars and board feet. Are such questions now confronting the Eskimo? If we could organize learning in Eskimo schools for survival in salmon fishing and gathering Native foods, we could design social studies which might save our own dwindling open space, and teach ourselves and our children how to live humanly in cities.

The final goal for evaluation—education for emotional health—is essential for Native people's survival, as it is for ours, to gain an appreciation of cultural ways so that we all may retain our balance in modern life. Sophistication and appreciation of cultural values are essential to anyone for making wise choices in acculturation. What should be kept, what should be modified, and what can be given away without loss, all determine the vitality and strength of Indian or Eskimo groups and their resilience in surviving in modern technological surroundings that can destroy them as people—as it is destroying the diversity of our dominant society.

Do public school social studies teach toward emotional health in the cities? Do social studies teach ways of renewing exhausted psyches? Is the present social and economic dropout rate and alienation the result of the failure of education to train us to survive in what has come to be an unbearable circumstance? The success of Indian education certainly depends on cultural and emotional survival as surely as it does for White students who must learn to live in Chicago, Detroit, and San Francisco as adequately as on the cattle ranges of Colorado. The critical need for any Indian student is to master the stress of modern life by achieving values that offer personal definition, human community, gratification from work, and faith in his own integrity—these are the needs of all students. So in this final sophistication, the Native American student is not alone in his mental health needs.

For the same reason, teachers in any classroom are not isolated from the challenge of working with Indian children, for the accomplishment is basically the nurturing and developing of the whole child—every child. The perspective of solutions sketched in this conclusion are of two dimensions—the humanly near and the politically far. This action view includes changing the structures that perpetuate negative schooling, and politically this means also meeting the challenges of changing the society that so many schools are frantically trying to preserve.

Certainly, in the overall view, this is a long-range revolution that frustrates many teachers absorbed in their daily schoolroom world. What can he or she do to even change the administration within his or her own school? On short terms, possibly nothing beyond the voting duties of a citizen. Militant teachers too frequently turn away from schools because "you can't teach humanly in this kind of a society." The view we are dealing with here is *out* of the classroom into the default of this phase of history. We can leave the classroom and enter the power struggle, or as frequently we can succumb to numbing withdrawal that stops teachers from doing even what little they can do in their own classrooms. There can be another focus because the children are there. If we shifted our view into the individual destiny of each student, what could a teacher realistically see and do to promote whole child development?

As a teacher in a classroom we can do little about the policy, or even the necessity, of sending Eskimo children thousands of miles away to finish high school, yet we can deal with this reality in the classroom. How?

Empathetically we can appreciate the personality needs of the students who must make the educational journey. We know they will need clear identity. We know they will need great resources within to make this experience positive. The Eskimo students setting forth need what all our children need, a strong foundation of self and culture to stand on. In some fashion, each teacher is contributing to or

Visiting seniors from the bilingual and bicultural St. Mary's High School on the Yukon dance for the students of Bethel's Consolidated Elementary and High School. A dancer from St. Mary's village teaches and leads this dance of Eskimo life.

negating this process, perhaps concurrently doing both! The teacher has broad freedom in person-to-person learning and communication. On significant levels, education results from interpersonal success and this can be accomplished even in the midst of repressive administration.

This writing touches on many self-fulfilling failures between teachers and students. Most of these failures are culturally imposed and would be there whether administrations changed or not. These defaults will remain until we learn to equalize our cultural stations and minimize the power discrepancies of ethnic discrimination. Until this happens teachers and students will remain isolated by the chasm that divides them, though teachers will go on struggling to reach across the gulf to the different child.

Bibliography

Anderson, H. Dewey, and Walter Crosby Eells, 1935, *Alaska Natives: A Survey of Their Sociological and Educational Status.* Stanford, Calif.: Stanford University Press.

Barnhardt, Raymond John, 1970, *Qualitative Dimensions in the Teaching of American Indian Children: A Descriptive Analysis of the Schooling Environment in Three North Pacific Coast Indian Communities.* Doctoral dissertation, University of Oregon.

Bateson, Gregory, and Margaret Mead, 1942, *Balinese Character: A Photographic Analysis.* New York: New York Accademy of Sciences.

Benedict, Ruth, 1934, *Patterns of Culture.* Boston: Houghton Mifflin Company.

Birdwhistell, Ray L., 1970, *Kinesics and Context.* Philadelphia: University of Pennsylvania Press.

Collier, John, Jr., 1967, *Visual Anthropology: Photography as a Research Method.* New York: Holt, Rinehart and Winston, Inc.

Dumont, Robert V., Jr., 1971, "Learning English and How to be Silent; Studies in American Indian Classrooms," in *The Functions of Language in the Classroom,* Courtney B. Cazden *et al.,* eds. New York: Teachers College Press.

Fuchs, Estelle, and Robert J. Havighurst, 1972, *To Live on This Earth: American Indian Education.* New York: Doubleday & Company, Inc.

Hall, Edward T., 1959, *The Silent Language.* New York: Doubleday & Company, Inc.

————, 1966, *The Hidden Dimension.* New York: Doubleday & Company, Inc.

Havighurst, Robert J., and Bernice L. Neugarten, 1954, *American Indian and White Children: A Sociopsychological Investigation.* Chicago: University of Chicago Press.

Hippler, Arthur E., 1970, *A Selected Annotated Bibliography of Alaskan and Other Eskimo Acculturation.* Institute of Social, Economic, and Government Research, SEG No. 28, August. College, Alaska: University of Alaska.

Jenness, Aylette, 1970, *Dwellers of the Tundra: Life in an Alaskan Eskimo Village,* with photographs by Jonathan Jenness. Toronto: Crowell-Collier Press.

Johnson, Broderick H., 1968, *Navaho Education at Rough Rock.* Rough Rock, Ariz.: D.I.N.E., Inc.

King, Richard A., 1967, *The School at Mopass: A Problem of Identity.* New York: Holt, Rinehart and Winston, Inc.

Lantis, Margaret, 1952, "Eskimo Herdsmen," In *Human Problems in Technological Change,* Edward Spicer, ed. New York: Russell Sage Foundation.

Mead, Margaret, and Paul Byers, 1967, *The Small Conference.* The Hague, N.V.: Mouton & Co.

Michael, Henry N., ed., 1967, *Lieutenant Zagoskin's Travels in Russian America, 1842–1844: The First Ethnographic and Geographic Investigations in the Yukon and Kuskokwim Valleys of Alaska.* Arctic Institue of North America, Anthropology of the North: Translations from Russian Sources No. 7. Toronto: University of Toronto Press.

Ong, Walter J., S. J., 1963 "Latin Language as a Renaissance Puberty Rite," in *Education and Culture: Anthropological Approaches,* George D. Spindler, ed. New York: Holt, Rinehart and Winston, Inc.

Oswalt, Wendell H., 1963*a*, *Mission of Change in Alaska: Eskimos and Moravians on the Kuskokwim.* San Marino, Calif.: Huntington Library Publications.

————, 1963*b, Napaskiak: An Alaskan Eskimo Community.* Tucson, Ariz.: University of Arizona Press.

Parkman, Francis, 1898, *The Jesuits in North America.* Boston: Little, Brown & Company.

Ray, Charles K., 1959, *A Program of Education for Alaskan Natives: A Research Report,* rev. ed. College, Alaska: University of Alaska.

Schwalbe, Anna Buxbaum, 1951, *Dayspring on the Kuskokwim: The Story of Moravian Missions in Alaska.* Bethlehem, Pa.: Moravian Press.

Schweitzer, Albert, 1949, *Out of My Life and Thought.* New York: Holt, Rinehart and Winston, Inc.

Spindler, George D., 1963, "Education Among the Menomini," in *Education and Culture: Anthropological Approaches,* George and Louise Spindler, eds. New York: Holt, Rinehart and Winston, Inc.

U.S. Congress, 1969, *Indian Education, 1969.* Hearings before the Subcommittee on Indian Education of the Committee on Labor and Public Welfare of the U.S. Senate, 91st Congress, First Session, Part 1.

Wax, Murray, 1971, *Indian American: Unity and Diversity.* Englewood Cliffs, N.J.: Prentice-Hall, Inc.

————, and Rosalie H. Wax, 1964, "Cultural Deprivation as an Educational Ideology." *Journal of American Indian Education* 3:2 (January), pp. 15–18.

————, ————, and Robert V. Dumont, Jr., 1964, *Formal Education in the American Indian Community.* Monograph No. 1 (supplement, *Social Problems* XI:4), Society for the Study of Social Problems. Garden City, N.Y.: Adelphi College.

Wolcott, Harry F., 1967, *A Kwakiutl Village and School.* New York: Holt, Rinehart and Winston, Inc.

————, 1969, *The Teacher as an Enemy.* Eugene, Oregon: Center for the Advanced Study of Educational Administration (mimeographed).